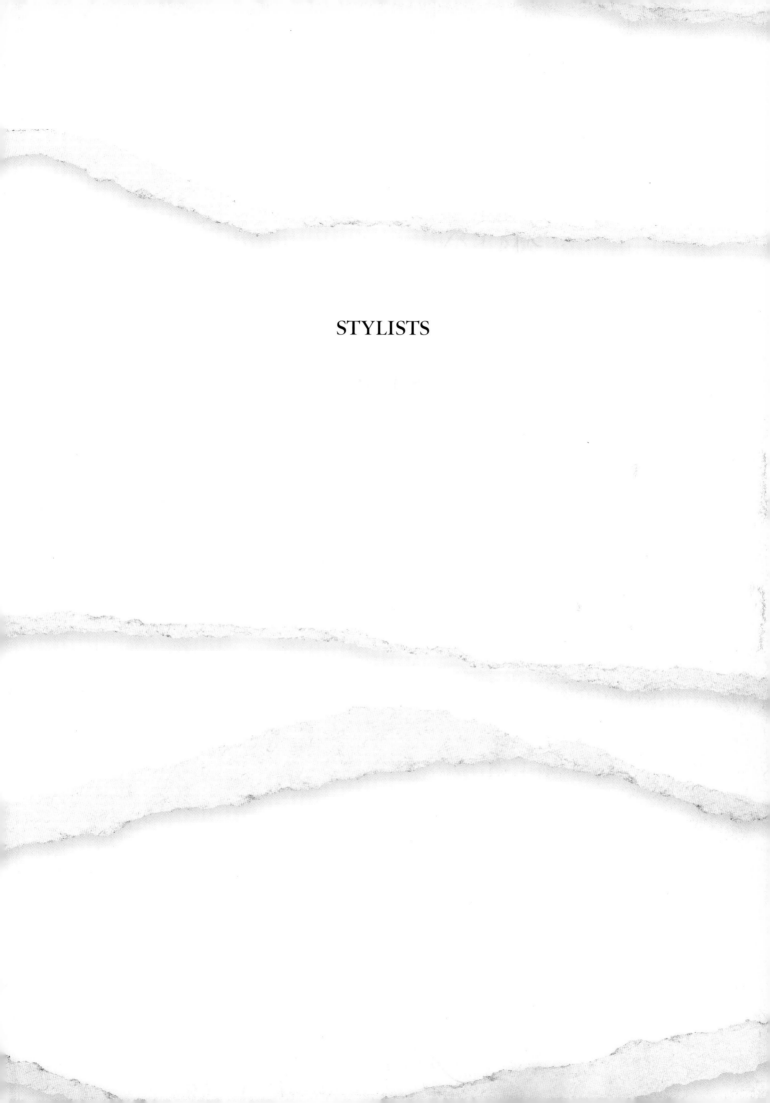

STYLISTS

STYLISTS

NEW FASHION VISIONARIES
BY KATIE BARON

LAURENCE KING PUBLISHING

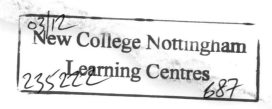

LAURENCE KING

Published in 2012
by Laurence King Publishing Ltd
361–373 City Road
London EC1V 1LR
United Kingdom
Tel: + 44 20 7841 6900
Fax: + 44 20 7841 6910
email: enquiries@laurenceking.com
www.laurenceking.com

This book was produced by
Laurence King Publishing Ltd, London

ISBN: 978 1 85669 829 0

Commissioning Editor: Helen Rochester
Senior Editor: Zoe Antoniou
Picture Researcher: Evi Peroulaki
Design by Micha Weidmann Studio

Printed in China

Frontispiece: From 'Pure Wonder', styled by
Tabitha Simmons, photographed by Craig McDean
for *Vogue Italia*, March 2008 (see page 167).

Contents

Foreword by Nick Knight

Page 7
From the story 'Galliano's Warriors', for the Summer/ Autumn 2007 issue of *Arena Homme Plus*, styled by Simon Foxton, photographed by Nick Knight. The image was featured in 'When You're a Boy', Foxton's groundbreaking retrospective held at The Photographers' Gallery, London, in 2009.

I realized, around fifteen or twenty years ago, that fashion had a much bigger voice than it perhaps recognized. At times, it has allowed itself to be trivialized, even scandalized, but, in the same way that music in the 1960s found that it had a political voice beyond just singing love songs, fashion has become an incredibly strong voice for change.

Stylists, wedded to the worlds of image-making and fashion – worlds that are the best mirrors we have for reflecting what society considers beautiful – have become some of the most significant agents of that change. For the great stylists now need to be viewed as a new level of designer: just as good and just as important within the context of shaping fashion as any designer, but with fewer commercial shackles – making them even more exciting, more audacious and, for me, more addictive to work with.

This is not a generation of stylists who are simply the people that get movie stars' clothes. In the same way, they are not just the people trying to convey what was shown on the catwalk in every story, even when they were responsible for that catwalk look in the first place. That has all changed.

Fashion film and live broadcasts online have brought the luxury of access to the once private factory of fashion ideas, along with a newfound notoriety amid the thrill of performance.

Above all, though, it is about fantasy and the places where the very best stylists can take you.

For me, an interesting thing happens when you go into the studio. You leave all the rules at the door – the ways of behaving and what is accepted as normal and not normal. It is the total acceptance of fantasy.

Unfortunately, over the last year or so I have spent a lot of time at memorial services in huge churches and cathedrals, but, while there, it occurred to me that once upon a time these buildings were a way of allowing the public to dream, to have fantasies. These huge frescoes and wall paintings and massive cascading statues were the cinema of the time, the agents of imagination, as fashion is now becoming.

People enjoy fantasy. They enjoy the freedom it suggests and the proposition of a different life. Stylists are just as responsible for that as anyone else in history.

What is it that makes a great – the greatest – stylist? It is imagination, a love and an understanding of fashion and a desire to see things that are not there. Like an amazing film, a great stylist will open your eyes to a world you had not – or could not possibly have – imagined. In the business of image-making there is nothing more exciting.

Introduction

Few professions have the ability to straddle as many areas of the industry in which they sit as fashion styling – an inherently modern, connective role whose elastic remit sees those who take it on potentially enveloped in every stage of the creative process. There was a time when stylists were all but invisible to the world beyond fashion's inner circle, only privately applauded, shielded behind the façades of the magazines, shows, advertising campaigns, music labels and design ateliers whose creative output they had been integral to shaping. But, a steadily growing shift in the dynamics of the fashion industry has given license to a special breed of entrepreneurial visionaries who have bridged the nebulous boundaries between art, culture and commerce to become not only the interpreters but also the originators of fashion.

Anchored in collaboration, a stylist's lifeblood is his or her ability to breathe co-conceived life into a central vision. It is these inspired meetings – the seminal partnerships and incendiary collaborations with photographers, designers, directors and artists – that this book explores, revealing some of the most significant examples of creative alchemy in modern fashion history.

Responsible for some of the most enduring images, ideas and trends within fashion's pantheon, the stylist offers a unique set of perspectives, providing a masterclass in mould-breaking innovation. Frequently delivering inspiration, information and transformation, the work of these influential creatives has been instrumental in developing the lexicon of both fashion and, by default, contemporary culture as we know it.

A celebration of contemporary styling, via a series of original interviews and a vast range of visual material, this book delivers an extensive insight into the pioneering work of an elite group of international stylists. From catwalk shows to music videos, from art direction to design, from editorial imagery to fine art, and including those who are also now editors, publishers, photographers, designers and directors in their own right, captured within these pages are some of fashion's most visionary thinkers and extraordinary communicators.

Page 8
Iconic model Hannelore Knuts, for the Summer 2005 issue of *10* magazine. Styled by Sophia Neophitou-Apostolou, in a 'power pose', which is typical of the stylist's work. Photographed by Greg Lotus.

CHRISTIANE ·ARP

Christiane Arp

Page 11

From the April 2010 issue of German *Vogue*, photographed by one of Arp's closest long-term collaborators, Peter Lindbergh.

'The biggest thrill for me as an editor? To be able to create, on the back of my own ideas, a hype,' declares Christiane Arp, the formidable editor-in-chief and fashion director of German *Vogue*. Her love of craftsmanship and her well-honed understanding of the powerful cultural affirmations at play within a strong fashion image have arguably redefined the magazine for a contemporary audience.

Pushing boundaries and taking risks to remain relevant ('If you think it's right, it's probably already wrong,' she suggests) is stock-in-trade for Arp, who has used her decade-long tenure at the magazine to cultivate relationships that have put the magazine back into a global frame of reference. 'I love to have the idea that through something that I do I can influence women to have a certain strength, and if fashion is a tool for that then wonderful,' says Arp. 'But knowledge is a tool as well. It's not only about running a magazine that provides you with high-quality beautiful pictures but also to give you an idea about the way you feel, to inspire.'

Arp's expertise comes from being a veteran of magazine culture, having been initiated into the publishing arena in the early 1980s, interning at now-defunct knitting magazine *Nicole*. The magazine's strong photographic bent, and an editor that educated her in every aspect from layouts to print production, gave her an appetite for magazines that shifted her focus for good from a degree in fashion design. 'It was, when I look at myself today, the base of everything I needed,' Arp recalls. The magazine folded in 1988, during the heyday of the supermodels, when the frenzy for fashion photography was hitting fever pitch.

Next up was the fashion and lifestyle magazine *Viva*, and Arp's crucial submersion, as fashion editor, in a project built from scratch. Though influential, its run only lasted two years, but it afforded Arp the brand new magazine, in 1993, that was to galvanize her career: *Amica*. As fashion director, working alongside publisher Dirk Manthey, Arp spent two years developing the title into Germany's new fashion and lifestyle magazine for women. The blank canvas gave Arp the chance to craft her vision in the most holistic, entrepreneurial sense.

'He came in and we had nothing, not even a desk,' recounts Arp, who recalls the time as one of the most defining in her career. 'Dirk would say things like "fly to the moon and do something there", and then I understood. No borders. And that was, for me, the most inspiring thing. I stopped looking at other magazines because I wanted to find my own way to approach fashion, photography and even printing again. In between we had a huge fight and he [Dirk] said, "Okay Christiane, you do what you think is right. If it's successful then I'll never interfere. If not, we have to talk." Lucky me, it was successful.'

That brand of strong, independent thinking reflects a philosophy that Arp has maintained throughout her career, trading heavily on instinct and intuition. 'My career has never really been about the right or wrong business card,' states Arp. 'It's only ever been about what felt right.'

On taking the reins of German *Vogue* in 2002, Arp carried with her a similar fearlessness. The treatment of supermodel Claudia Schiffer, a regular cover model for the magazine, exemplifies the level of both national pride and progressive creativity that Arp has brought to its pages. While Schiffer continues to foster an international presence across a wealth of magazines, as testament to Arp's persuasive powers, it is German *Vogue* where she pushes her famously wholesome (albeit sexy) image into new territories. The June 2010 issue featured Schiffer naked while pregnant with her third child, while the June 2008 'Sex' issue, shot by Mario Testino, portrayed a 1940s-era dominatrix-style Schiffer in mask, suspenders and very little else. 'She's a woman that I really, really admire but it's a friendship as well. Claudia knows that I would never ever do anything that wouldn't be good for her and that's why I think I get everything from her. Her most beauty, her most loyalty... It's a strong bond between her and me and beyond that, Claudia Schiffer as a brand. Plus, of course, brand *Vogue*.'

A similar sense of hype came with the June 2009 issue that saw Arp feature Heidi Klum, at the height of the debate regarding her professional status/value, on both the cover and the four inside fashion stories. With Klum looking more high fashion than she had in years, it proved a double coup, raising the profile of both the magazine and model. The issue sold 30% more copies than usual.

Other allegiances with icons of German creative culture, nurtured by Arp, have also contributed to the skyrocketing profile of the brand's German arm. For the thirtieth anniversary issue of the magazine in 2009, she enlisted some of Germany's most influential cultural icons, Karl Lagerfeld, Peter Lindbergh and Bruce Weber (who has German forefathers), to present a visual extravaganza that would project a modern vision of Germany and its culture. Coinciding with the twenty-year anniversary of the reunification of Germany and the sixty-year anniversary of the birth of the state, it was a crucial project, with a cultural resonance beyond the usual remit. It was also the beginning of the recession. 'At the end of 2009, the magic word was crisis, which meant for me, for the first time being in full charge of a magazine, I faced an enormous challenge,' says Arp.

Arp's reaction, unheard of for an editor-in-chief, was to give all three complete creative freedom, commissioning each one to work on a separate (black, red and gold) edition of the issue. According to photographer Peter Lindbergh, 'She is one of the very few people I've met who understands that a fashion magazine today should be an instrument to define our culture and be more than a catalogue for the fashion industry.' While Lagerfeld and Lindbergh shot in Berlin, Weber shot in New York and Montauk, USA. All three set out to explode outdated cultural myths and to reveal a new and celebratory perspective. 'I lost my fear at that moment,' reveals Arp. 'We were in this powerful position to just do something and not stand still – grabbing the chance to convince everybody that the only chance that we have is to move on. It says something about the essence of our country, which to me is my idea of the perfect *Vogue*.'

Despite having an international pool of world-class talent at her fingertips, which comes from being a *Vogue* editor, Arp maintains a strong link with new German talent also. Photographers Patrick Bienert and Max von Gumppenberg are newcomers to the magazine, while fledgling designer Michael Sontag is also firmly on her radar.

It is the ideal of connective hands-on craftsmanship, however, that continues to drive her daily. 'Putting together a magazine is fundamentally about craftsmanship. These little bits and pieces, finding the right thing, the right buttons – that is what I still love,' states Arp. 'I still want to be there, styling – actually dressing the girls myself. We must never lose our first love.'

Christiane Arp

Page 14
Four German *Vogue* covers illustrating Arp's mastery of the magazine as a tool for both personal and cultural reinvention. Clockwise from top left: Heidi Klum, photographed by Francesco Carrozzini, June 2009; a heavily pregnant Claudia Schiffer, photographed by Karl Lagerfeld, June 2010; young superstar model Frida Gustavassion, photographed by Greg Kadel for the 'Trends' issue, March 2010; Claudia Schiffer, photographed by Mario Testino for the 'Sex' issue, June 2008.

Page 15
Karl Lagerfeld's portrait of Bill Kaulitz – the distinctive lead singer of German rock-pop band Tokio Hotel – for the October 2009 issue of German *Vogue*.

Pages 16–17
The fashionable renaissance of Heidi Klum, photographed by Francesco Carrozzini for the June 2009 issue of German *Vogue*.

CAMILLE BIDAULT-WADDINGTON

**Camille
Bidault-Waddington**

Page 19
A characteristically
irreverent image
for the Autumn/Winter
2008 issue of *Purple
Fashion Magazine*,
photographed by one of
Bidault-Waddington's
original, and most
significant consorts,
Horst Diekgerdes.

To familiarize yourself with Camille Bidault-Waddington's work is to get to know Bidault-Waddington herself. Or, at least, the playful, self-referencing perspective that magazines – *AnOther Magazine*, *Self Service*, *Purple Fashion Magazine* – and fashion labels – Marc by Marc Jacobs, Chloé and Sonia Rykiel – have all found so alluring. Irreverent, rich with spontaneity and pulled together from a bricolage of stream-of-consciousness-style ideas, the natural charm of a Bidault-Waddington image stands miles away from the chic but often fierce rigour of so many of her Parisian contemporaries.

Unconcerned with etiquette and typified by retro-influenced accents, Bidault-Waddington's aesthetic spins around a sensual, uninhibited flamboyance that has managed to eclipse those grounded in more rigid preoccupations, and position her among the styling elite. 'Behind the façade of the perfect style that Camille can provide there is always something mysterious, always sexual,' says Olivier Zahm, founder and editor-in-chief of *Purple Fashion Magazine*. 'But it's not in the style of Agent Provocateur, it doesn't have to have a sign on it, what she does is much more beautiful and subtle than that.'

Born in Normandy and having originally studied graphic design, whose prospects she dismissed as 'too boring, to be honest', she enrolled in Studio Berçot in Paris, on a fashion course where, she recalls, 'they teach nothing technical, but more how to open your eyes and look at things'. When, in 1993, *Vogue Paris* came calling for an assistant, the fashion college sent Bidault-Waddington, and her metamorphosis into professional stylist began.

While assisting there, she began collaborating with photographer Horst Diekgerdes, moving with him to London in 1997 and establishing vital links with a group of key innovators: stylists Katie Grand and Katy England, and photographer Phil Poynter, who were shaping London's explosive new editorial scene. 'At that time in London you could do anything,' explains Bidault-Waddington. 'It was really good because you could wrap bits of fabric, you could put clothes upside down – especially at *Dazed & Confused* – the more creative the better. It was perfect for me.'

A stint with Grand at *The Face* followed, before a return to Paris in 2001 and her involvement with the inaugural season of Marc Jacobs' highly successful Marc by Marc Jacobs range, a line she still works on. It is a label in which her distinctive bohemian touch still resonates loudly – exemplified by the consistent use of playful colour, unpretentious elegance and a host of retro-modern inflections. French label Sonia Rykiel, for whom Bidault-Waddington has consulted since 2009, is similarly invested with her infectious, coltish charm. The styling of the Spring/Summer 2011 show borrowed from the 1970s, channelling shades of summer on the Côte d'Azur, but the accent was modern and the translation bound to Bidault-Waddington's gift for assembling eclectic references with complete fluency.

Unlike other stylists, who in their consulting capacity are employed to get busy on the specifics of hemlines and lapel widths in order to hit sales, Bidault-Waddington has a role that revolves around generating the right mood, nailing the transient but crucial nuances of the bigger picture. 'For me, it's just not essential to be that precise,' she affirms. Zahm attests to this: 'To me, to be French is about love and life and sex, and fashion is just a way to celebrate those things. Camille always does that and with a special playfulness. What she does is feel the mood of fashion.'

Part of Bidault-Waddington's appeal springs directly from her take-it-or-leave-it attitude. She is happy to be perceived as unorthodox and is unconcerned with standard protocol. 'I just do it for me, it's very selfish really. If I'm honest, I don't really give a fuck what people are thinking in the end,' she declares, while also confessing to having had an 'aversion to luxury labels'. The benefit to her portfolio of clients, of course, is an image, or a collection, full of integrity and originality and consequently – if you buy into Bidault-Waddington's personal perspective – unlikely to disappoint. Indeed, she insists that she 'is not intellectual, about anything', instead relying on instinct and an absolute clarity in terms of knowing what she does and does not like.

Creative heroes and stylistic influences, unsurprisingly, have a similarly unconventional bent. Bidault-Waddington describes the late artist Louise Bourgeois as an inspiration 'for being like a woman but thinking like a man. There's something very powerful about not being a girly woman – androgynous. I quite like the people who don't think with their gender so much.' The similarly iconic non-conformist, the late writer and raconteur Quentin Crisp also features as a stylistic influence. 'It's really important to be disturbed, I think,' suggests Bidault-Waddington. 'To think: that's exciting, that's weird or disturbing, or even that you don't understand it. To consider something to be really freaky horrible and then one minute afterwards find you really love it, is important.'

Driven by the challenge of that eternal creative restlessness, Bidault-Waddington is also following in the footsteps of Venetia Scott, her colleague on the Marc by Marc Jacobs range, by moving behind the camera herself. Shooting mostly for *Purple Fashion Magazine*, she claims that it will not devour her passion for styling but that it has given her a new outlet to liberate her constantly roving eye, which she loves. 'At the beginning you have an idea that you think is precise but you can't really explain it and of course the photographer has his own ideas too,' she explains. 'The result can be really good but it's never really the thing you wanted.'

Although she does occasionally photograph models, she says she prefers to shoot her friends, declaring that 'if you put a real person in it, it often works because it becomes quite sentimental'. Many would suggest, however, that it is her ability to pour the very essence of her models into the characters they temporarily inhabit that exemplifies her skill, for Bidault-Waddington's women are indeed a unique breed. Whether it is model Eniko Mihalik strutting through downtown New York in a gold brocade dress, a girl wearing little else but a pair of leather dungarees or model Elise Crombez swathed in layers wandering through the late-afternoon sunlight (a favourite shoot of hers), every one is utterly convincing. Zahm agrees: 'When Camille styles a girl, it looks like it could be her life, as if she was always ready for you. She [the model] is there as herself and to give herself to the picture. It's more than fashion – it's someone that you want in life.'

Returning to the question of how close fact and fiction sit within her images, even she cannot confirm entirely. 'They were me for a long time. Actually, they're probably still all me. It's not that I adore myself and sometimes I don't even notice. Sometimes the girl can be blonde and wearing an evening dress but there is something there that it seems is obviously me. But since I don't know exactly what I'm doing, it must... I must project something.'

Camille Bidault-Waddington

Page 22

Top left: From the Spring/Summer 2005 issue of *Self Service*, photographed by Ellen Von Unwerth, which bears all the hallmarks of Bidault-Waddington's idiosyncratically sexy styling. Top right: One of a series of photographs by Terry Richardson for the Spring/Summer 2006 issue of *Self Service*, which Bidault-Waddington describes as both her favourite and most emotional of shoots. Bottom: From a story for Italian women's magazine *Io Donna*, photographed by Bidault-Waddington.

Page 23

Model Iris Strubegger, photographed by Glen Luchford for the Spring/Summer 2010 issue of *Purple Fashion Magazine*. The image captures the subtly provocative essence of the stylist's work.

Pages 24–25

A typically retro-inflected image from a story by photographer Glen Luchford for the Autumn/Winter 2009 issue of *AnOther Magazine*.

JUDY·BLAME

Page 27
Blame's typically
outré styling lavished
on Princess Julia – a
countercultural icon of
London's club scene in
the 1980s, which became
the breeding ground for
Blame's wild creativity.
Photographed by
Mark Lebon.

Page 29
This series of editorial
images illustrate Blame's
consistently subversive
approach to fashion
styling. Top left and
bottom right: From the
'Black Magic' story,
for i-D magazine's
'Obsession' issue, August
1997, photographed by
Mark Mattock.
Top right: Blame styling
one of his own creations
– a headband for
fashion designer Carlos
Miele – photographed
by Eddie Monsoon for
i-D, May 2001. Bottom
left: More of Blame's
characteristically
imaginative DIY styling
for a story entitled
'Punk', for i-D,
June 2009.

Pages 30–31
From Blame's visually
anarchic work, for the
'Punk' story, for i-D.

According to Judy Blame, 'Shock doesn't last very long. Surprise is always good. And fun? If you're having fun it will always show in the picture.' And Blame is a man who should know, for it is his unorthodox, hands-on approach to fashion, and a career that bridges the fashion, music and design industries, that has been instrumental in defining the very essence of styling as a profession in its own right. Drawing from a vast palette of visual culture, Blame epitomizes the magpie-like life of a stylist and covers the huge creative ground that only the most talented can.

Blame's story, and his legacy to fashion (so far), is predominantly a tale of the deification of street style. From the DIY glamour of the London club scene of the 1980s, where he acquired his name ('a lot of us changed our names back then – to fit the image, not the person'), right up to his current jewellery collection in Rei Kawakubo's Dover Street Market, Blame has provided a pivotal, celebratory re-imagining of grass-roots fashion.

That language, derived from Blame's life-long obsession with the visual arts, was triggered at the age of five, when his family moved from the sleepy English countryside to the comparative visual fantasia of 1960s Madrid. 'Out of all the children, I was the one who loved the bull-fight, who loved the art. If my mother went shopping in Madrid, she would drop me at the Prado Museum and pick me up three hours later. As an eight-year-old kid, being able to walk around and see all the Goyas and the Velázquezs, I was in heaven. I've always had a thing for absorbing visual culture. It was an incredible source of entertainment for me. I realized very early on how powerful visuals are.'

The family moved back to England in the 1970s, and Blame's self-taught creativity and love of the instant gratification that came with cus-tomization piqued when punk exploded. 'It was an explosion and I really needed to be near wherever that was,' explains Blame, 'but the main thing about that was that there was a sound and a visual. The packaging. The record sleeves. The badges. It was kind of homemade in a way and that really appealed to me.'

Punk's inherently aggressive nature and the lack of camaraderie made it a short-lived love affair, but the notion of a cultural movement fuelled by a convergence of sound, visuals and fashion did kick-start a new cre-ative romance. A move to Manchester, a city also heaving with a burgeon-ing music scene, and which Blame refers to as his 'true college', brought friendships with some of Britain's most important nascent innovators, in-cluding record-industry graphic designers Malcolm Garrett and Peter Sav-ille. It was the unorthodox, creative tribe Blame had been latently seeking out and the time when his disparate vision began to coalesce. 'I've always had a passion for the way people look, what they look at, and also what they sound like,' says Blame. 'The entire thing became a huge a passion. Styling is a passion.'

By the mid-1980s, the group had moved back to London. Where punk was subsiding, the New Romantic movement was rising fast, and Blame was in a major phase of creation, sculpting jewellery from scavenged objects to go clubbing in. 'We were going out wearing these wild pieces of jewelry and I had no concept of it being anything other than an outfit in itself,' recalls Blame. When Antony Price, the designer behind Bryan Ferry's look on the *Roxy Music* album, started commissioning him to create original pieces, it sealed his direction. 'It was peacock time and we were all finding our own visual language. Antony was the perfect person for me because what he'd been doing for Bryan was so glam. I learned a lot from him about lighting and make-up and putting on a show.'

London also brought the 'New London, New York' show – an exhibition curated by the infamous New York club promoter Susanne Bartsch, which took the feral London talents of Blame, milliner Stephen Jones, designer John Richmond and performance artist Leigh Bowery to be showcased in New York. It shifted the dynamics of their underground scene, profiles rose swiftly, and, for Blame, styling for magazines such as *i-D* and *The Face* became regular gigs. Blame's vision of cut-and-paste fashion was becoming increasingly influential and, in 1985, he and fellow designer, the late Christopher Nemeth, opened a store called The House of Beauty & Culture. With the convergence of fashion and music becoming so close as to be almost inseparable, it was a magnet for clubbers, fashion addicts and wannabe pop stars desperate to bask in the attention that surrounded their avant-garde styling, and the ideal place for Blame to flex his conceptual craft.

Boy George, whom Blame met in a club, was a significant high-profile pioneer of Blame's bespoke oversized pieces of jewellery, but it was Neneh Cherry (whom Blame also met in a club through mentor Ray Petri), followed by Massive Attack, that were to prove most seminal. Blame took on the role of full creative director for them, cultivating directional image-led personas that swept across music videos, TV performances and editorial imagery. His stylistic guidance not only defined those artists for a generation hungry (as Blame had been) for the full package of sound, style and attitude, but also changed Blame's own creative process. 'It was my job to find the photographer, the clothes, everything,' says Blame. 'Juergen Teller's first music work came through me. It was from working with people like Neneh that I realized that I was in fact educating other people.'

That expertise has been recognized by a number of others who have employed his talents – John Galliano, Comme des Garçons, even high-street retailer Uniqlo – and Blame has remained resolutely steeped in an irreverent, infectious flamboyance in each case. The creation of a customized denim range for Louis Vuitton in 2007 is a classic example of Blame's low-fi aesthetic reaching way beyond its original underground audience, with very little of the compromises that most designers are expected to make. In an unprecedented coup for both parties, creative director Marc Jacobs put the label's luxury ateliers at Blame's disposal, enabling him to 'mass-produce' bespoke pieces.

'We're great at taking lots of cultural references and splicing things together,' says Blame. 'It's very eclectic, the British sense of style. Eclectic, not eccentric, whereas I think I'm probably bordering on both. I've never been big on tradition, though, because I'm always breaking it – whether I know it or not.'

Reference remains key. In a cavernous basement space in east London, which Blame uses as a studio, is a pool table covered with rows of pristine books. Each one is neatly filled with dozens of images, a vast encyclopaedia of fashion impulses, which Blame refers to as his current visual dictionary. It is clear evidence that, decades on, his visual antenna is as acute as ever. 'Work has always saved me,' says Blame in grateful acknowledgement of the power of creativity amid a tumultuous lifestyle that, at times, almost killed him. 'And now I'm looking forward, too.'

DAVID BRADSHAW

'A successful image is one that everybody admires – whether they're male, female, straight or gay. It's easy to impress the people sitting either side of you at a fashion show. It's much harder to affect the people out there walking up and down the street and that's my challenge,' states David Bradshaw, one of the most industrious men in fashion.

Should it be possible to objectively proclaim an individual as *the* authority on style, the title would likely go to Bradshaw; the accidental stylist, design consultant and creative director whose perfectly considered perspective on fashion has, over the course of more than two decades, artfully helped guide a profusion of influential brands into various states of heightened desirability. It is a bold statement but one that is affirmed by a CV that kicks off with *Arena* magazine in the early 1990s (subsequently annexed by *Arena Homme Plus*), and goes on to notch up creative director and then editor of British *GQ Style*. It further details a series of enduring consultancies for such global fashion linchpins as Katharine Hamnett, Jil Sander, Calvin Klein (for whom Bradshaw was once placed on an unprecedented one-season exclusive contract), Miu Miu, Prada, Tom Ford, Alexander McQueen and Roland Mouret (for the new menswear collection Roland Mouret MR.).

Beyond personal achievement, his impressive trajectory also bears witness to how designers, with the assistance of external creative direction, have come to recognize the vital importance of forging brand illusions. The ability to contextualize design, to spin a collection into a full lifestyle fantasy, is a skill that Bradshaw, as his stack of heavyweight clients can attest to, works better than any other. 'David has a very real, strong identity,' states Mouret. 'Beyond the fact that he's possibly the most stylish man I've ever seen, I was attracted to the values and the person because it's that kind of strength of identity that will be able to project something additional on to my work.'

With a naturally analytical approach to everything he does (a legacy of his initial training as an engineer) and a perfectly honed creative instinct, Bradshaw has become an expert in distilling brand messages. However, his route to success was anything but obvious. Having been introduced to the world of fashion by illustrator John Babbidge (for whom Bradshaw used to sit), his first foray into styling came when, in order to sell advertising space for now-defunct magazine *Unique*, he would persuade the owners of London's most directional independent boutiques to place adverts in exchange for shoot credits. He would then dress the models on the shoots himself purely to ensure his clients got the required trade-off. This early engagement with the business of fashion, grafting his way into a position with prospects, was the cornerstone on which his unique combination of creative intuition and shrewd cultural acumen was founded.

'I think my career, like for a lot of people, particularly people from my background, is about survival in the first instance,' declares Bradshaw in reference to his youth growing up in south London. 'Making the most of one's opportunity and trying to make sense of a world in which you have no guide or mentor. A door opens, you have a look inside and if it's interesting you make sure it doesn't close behind you. It's about striking a claim for some kind of relevance.'

Styling gave Bradshaw exactly that sense of relevance, with a catalogue shoot styling footwear for a high-street retailer and the launch of independent men's magazine *Arena* (created by Nick Logan, founder of *The Face*) sealing its status, for him, as a viable profession. It was 1990 and the start of his now-legendary nine-year tenure at *Arena*, during which time, working alongside the genius of other on-staff innovators such as

David Bradshaw

Page 41
A classic example of
the modern edge that
Bradshaw brings to
traditional menswear.
Photographed by Chad
Pitman for the Spring/
Summer 2009 issue of
British *GQ Style*.

Page 42
Bradshaw channels
a sense of youthful
anarchy in the 'A Riot
of My Own' story, for
the Spring/Summer
2007 issue of British *GQ
Style*. Photographed by
Nathaniel Goldberg.

graphic designer Neville Brody and contributing photographers Juergen Teller and David Sims, Bradshaw rose from intern to creative director.

The *Arena* years coincided with a major groundswell of interest in menswear, which, combined with *Arena*'s pioneering mix of fashion, politics, sport and sex, made the magazine both a seminal reference for modern male culture and a catalyst for Bradshaw's personal emergence into the limelight. 'We were given a creative import beyond our years purely because there was no real hierarchy there,' explains Bradshaw of the creative democracy that made *Arena* so significant. 'There were other magazines but they were all owned or published by institutional publishing houses, so there wasn't that sense of independence or counterculture that we had.'

Bradshaw's debut collaboration with a designer came via Katharine Hamnett in 1992, transferring his editorial prowess into the design studio in the first in a series of collaborations centring on commercial development and creative intervention that have shaped his career. Working with Hamnett, Bradshaw learned the process of design and the invaluable role of creative interloper – unifying the designer, design team and collection. It was also the first time (of many) that Bradshaw was asked to turn his menswear expertise towards a womenswear collection.

A contract with another major force in contemporary fashion, Jil Sander, followed in 1996, closely tailed by Prada and Miu Miu in 1997 and Prada Sport in 1998 – placing Bradshaw in a role of intense creative development that spanned the entire brand spectrum from product to shows to campaign imagery. The relationship with Prada lasted for seven years and supplied Bradshaw with further validation of his own tough work ethic. 'I was exposed to the idea of rigour, of hard work that was way beyond just getting an image on a page or dressing a guy and making him look good,' recalls Bradshaw of his time working with the formidable Miuccia Prada. 'It's about not accepting the easy way out, not accepting the short route. It was hard, but such a good process in terms of teaching you how to apply your craft and your intelligence to something.'

By 2005, courtesy of the launch of *GQ Style*, Bradshaw was once again addressing the slippery issue of modern male culture within the publishing industry. His aim was to forge an identity that resonated with both those ensconced in the rarefied world of fashion and the average man on the street.

'As soon as you start talking about fashion and men, the vanity thing comes along and immediately turns off a lot of men – including editors and publishers,' says Bradshaw. 'Historically, however, vanity has been a major driving force in terms of creativity, and if you look at male magazines right now those that are focused on libido are diminishing, while those that are more concerned with vanity are increasing in popularity. It's all about contemporary masculinity, making it relevant, and I want to be as close to that conversation as possible.'

Others want to keep him close to that conversation, too, confirmed by a reappraisal, in 2007, of his role at Calvin Klein. Despite the legendary politics that surround the intimate relationship between designer and stylist, Italo Zucchelli, creative director of menswear at Calvin Klein, describes Bradshaw as, 'A groundbreaking men's stylist who has pushed boundaries, catapulting men's fashion into a new realm. Aside from having exceptional taste and amazing personal style, he is unpretentious, fun to work with and very exciting.'

When asked, as a veteran of high fashion, what it is that makes *him* excited, it seems that relevance is still high on his agenda. 'I still love the energy of new talent. I'm all about a progressive dialogue and I'm not looking for a cosy life. I need to skate around the pool of failure – of oblivion. In a way, I'm a believer in the Malcolm Gladwell [author of *Outliers: The Story of Success*] philosophy of having to do something over and over again,' he explains. 'It's about putting 10,000, 50,000 hours of work in and fundamentally there isn't an expert on the planet who hasn't done that.'

David Bradshaw

Page 43
Bradshaw shows just how wide he can stretch the remit of menswear, in 'The Edge of the World' story for the Spring/Summer 2010 issue of *GQ Style*. Photographed by Chad Pitman.

FRANCESCA BURNS

Pages 44–45
From a location
shoot in Utah for the
Spring/Summer 2011
issue of Australian
magazine, *Doing Bird*.
Photographed by
Angelo Pennetta.

'Being a stylist is fundamentally about having a very specific point of view on fashion. It's like sociology in lots of ways. Documenting a moment, social history', states Francesca Burns, the influential fashion director of *GQ Style* (Burns is the inaugural womenswear director of the magazine in its freshly reconfigured format), former fashion editor of *i-D*, contributing fashion editor of *Self Service, Purple Fashion Magazine,* Japanese *Vogue* and *Interview* magazines, as well as a panellist on the British Fashion Council's NewGen initiative, created to showcase new design talent.

Fuelled by the extraordinary power of fashion to both influence and reflect social evolution, Burns offers highly evocative images that present exactly those kinds of socio-fashion snapshots. With a rare potency – synonymous with the raw energy of youth and actively engaged in chasing beauty – every image is laced with just enough shades of reality to ensure that all flights of fashion fantasy are rooted in authenticity. 'I've always liked girls who feel like they have an essence of attainability – even if they're clearly amazing,' says Burns of her casting choices.

The notion of using the semblance of reality as a loose starting point from which to base the image-making fantasy (whether shooting American model Hannah Holman at her home in Utah or British supermodel Agyness Deyn in her back garden in Bolton for *i-D*'s 'Icon' issue – one of Burns' all-time favourite shoots) has underscored the trajectory of Burns' career to date, and comes from a first-hand understanding of the impact of fashion on every area of the cultural spectrum.

Born in Guildford, on the outskirts of London, Burns says that although, as a teenager, friends would often explain her to others in advance – forewarning them of her unconventional personal style – fashion was always a natural form of self-expression. 'I've always loved the fact that you could use fashion to create a language about yourself that was instantly communicable,' says Burns.

Later, after embarking on a degree in business at Royal Holloway College, one tutor (improbably named David Bowie) suggested she switch to something more creative after seeing the disconnection between the student and the relatively conservative course (Burns recalls that on her first day she turned up in a Vivienne Westwood kilt mini and her hair worked into a scorpion's tail curling back over her head). She promptly transferred to London College of Fashion and, courtesy of a seminal two-week work placement, began her fashion career by assisting William Baker, then creative director for Kylie Minogue.

Her first professional job was helping Baker on Minogue's now legendary 'Can't Get You Out of My Head' video, followed by her 'Fever' World Tour in 2002 – a role that triggered Burns' understanding of how to artfully reconcile the collision of street culture and high fashion, interweaving the fantasy and the reality in one cohesive package. 'It was a real culture clash,' says Burns. 'Film-makers and set designers, creatives of all kinds. William had brought in dancers from the Rambert Dance Company for the tour – people who had essentially given their entire lives to their craft, lots and lots of very inspiring people.' It also, according to Burns, instilled in her that true creativity was tethered intrinsically to the fact that 'there really is no set way of doing things'.

Stints assisting stylists Joe McKenna, Alex White and Jonathan Kaye followed before she became fashion editor for style bible *i-D*. Working with both established photographers such as Nick Knight, as well as those similarly on the ascendant such as Angelo Pennetta, Dan Jackson and Alasdair McLellan, Burns has been able to adopt a unique position as both a trendsetter and a reflective entity – inside the fashion industry's inner sanctum while still biting at the heels of all that is new, fresh and ultimately exciting.

The simultaneous brilliance of Burns, both inside and beyond the editorial world, and why she has proved so invaluable to brands such as Whistles, Twenty8Twelve, Mango and the department store Lane Crawford, for whom she has been instrumental on numerous campaigns, is that her vision revolves less around the notion of redefinition than it does around revelation. Hers is a language of amplification – of deifying previously unchampioned beauty and making the initially pleasing appear extraordinary. 'I always want things to be just a step outside reality, to create a fantasy situation by finding that perfect thing,' says Burns. 'But I'm primarily interested in the idea that fashion should communicate an identity. My work is about reacting to an emotional situation.' The shifts may not be seismic, but the subtle attitudinal about-turns are more than enough to deliver the kind of vitality and contemporary relevance that has made her a major player at a young age.

At present, Burns' work remains characterized by the apparently intimate moments she records, her most engaging stories always rooted in the close connections forged during the creative process. It is the documentation of a world constructed inside fashion's frame of reference, but wholly charged with the integrity of real experience.

Burns' answer, when asked what is the best part of being a professional stylist, echoes the infectiously heartfelt nature that visibly infiltrates all her work. 'It's really thrilling to be able to work with people that you feel that strongly about in the hope that you can communicate some of the beauty that you feel to a reader – or a bigger audience,' says Burns. 'Alasdair [McLellan] has a way of always finding that beauty in someone, for example. It's about real connections, the shared experiences, and the pictures are moments of that.'

Francesca Burns

Pages 48–49
More images from the Utah-based story for *Doing Bird*, which illustrate Burn's heartfelt one-step-removed-from-reality approach to fashion.

Pages 50–51
From Burn's definitive shoot for *i-D*'s celebrated May 2008 'Icon' issue, featuring noughties supermodel Agyness Deyn in her own backyard. Photographed by Alasdair McLellan.

MARIE·CH AIX

PROENZA SCHOULER

PROENZA SCHOULER

Marie Chaix

Page 53

A characteristically experimental take on women's fashion from Chaix for the Autumn/ Winter 2009 issue of *AnOther Magazine*. Photographed by Sølve Sundsbø.

Page 54

From the 'Imaculée Séduction' story, for the April 2011 issue of *Vogue Paris*, photographed by Hans Feurer – one of Chaix's earliest creative idols.

Page 55

Top: From the 'Close-up' story, photographed by Richard Burbridge for *Vogue Italia*, April 2010, which perfectly showcases Chaix's talent for aligning diverse references. Bottom: From the Spring/ Summer 2011 campaign for New York design duo, Proenza Schouler, who describe Chaix as the 'all important tie-breaker in the [design] equation'.

Equally as eloquent in the language of street style as she is in haute couture, Marie Chaix has a magpie-like, transcultural approach to image-making that epitomizes the many worlds linked by the nexus of styling.

One of the most significant young stylists to have emerged since 2005, Chaix offers a unique combination of reference points steeped in both an adoration of high fashion – a legacy from her French upbringing – and a passion for experimentation – derived from her time studying in London. Now based in New York, 'for the energy of the city, the bright crisp blue sky and the mix of fashion with other disciplines', Chaix has a multilingual appreciation of the art of visual communication, which has helped her to traverse from the polish of *Vogue Paris* to the radical pages of *AnOther Magazine, Mixte, i-D* and *Self Service*. According to Lazaro Hernandez and Jack McCollough, the New York design team behind the cool-girl-chic fashion label Proenza Schouler, she is also 'the all-important tiebreaker in the equation', and their 'not-so-secret-anymore weapon'.

Growing up in Strasbourg, north-eastern France, in 1996 Chaix found herself inspired by 'an obsession with John Galliano', and moved to London to do an art foundation course at Central Saint Martins College of Art & Design. More excited by the notion of what could be done with fashion beyond the world of pure design, Chaix took up a degree in art and design instead. 'At the end of the day, styling comes from different things,' explains Chaix. 'For my final project, as it turned out, I actually created a magazine. I loved images, creating a visual message. It was a new course, based on merging creative disciplines, which made it problematic for some people to understand. But the problems we faced made me push harder and ultimately made me understand there are no limits.'

Her time at Central Saint Martins stretched her creative sensibilities to the brink in more ways than one, for it was also then that she was first introduced to the more experimental side of fashion that would later underscore her work as a stylist. 'I saw girls in the street in London who were wild and fearless, which I thought was amazing. To me, at that time, it was very exhilarating, the energy was great,' explains Chaix.

It brokered a significant shift in perspective for Chaix, coming from a country where high fashion not only means high culture but is also a major point of national pride – in 1998, a 300-model fashion show by Yves Saint Laurent was the finale of choice for the football world cup. 'It was really interesting for me to see what was happening in London, because in France we revere fashion to the extent that, in some circumstances, I guess it can be restrictive. I like that English people feel more as if they can subvert fashion,' says Chaix. 'I also like the sense of humour, or at least the ability not to take things too seriously, that people have in England.'

In 2000, however, she returned to Paris, taking her appetite for progressive fashion to the cult French style title *Self Service*, sliding her way straight in to an internship and staying for more than five years. Written in English, but orchestrated by a group of Paris-based creatives of several different nationalities, it provided the perfect resting place for Chaix's taste for visual culture laced with a hybrid spin.

In 2006, she went freelance, shooting her first story, still for *Self Service*, with then fledgling photographer Dan Jackson, and, by 2007, her reputation had built enough momentum that she was already shooting with the fashion heroes she had been watching from afar for years.

She describes photographer Hans Feurer, with whom she first shot for *Mixte* magazine in 2007, as 'totally living up to all my expectations'. Photographed from long range, the story involved a quintessentially dynamic, pseudo-reportage set piece from Feurer, concerning a powerful-looking model striding through a busy square. 'He'd worked with all the editors I'd admired and has a visual language that I've always loved – the long lens, the visual movement, the sense of life,' recalls Chaix. 'When I was looking at him I felt like I was actually being transported. The girl would be standing in the middle of a square, he'd be twenty feet away and as she walked he'd shout "Sexy Mama"! It was a very physical process and very exhilarating.'

It is a sense of female power and vitality, witnessed by Chaix growing up as a child in the 1980s, which she has seamlessly drafted into her own work – only this time fleshed out with her brand of experimental irreverence. 'I like to generate the feeling of that woman,' says Chaix. 'I really respond to the idea of the woman looking like she chose to look like that, not as if she's been dressed up. I do like it if it can be sometimes a bit out there, or quite extreme, but I always hope to have an element of reality so that the woman doesn't look silly or surreal. She should be a strong woman who remains beautiful.'

Her uncanny ability to channel that sexy, strong 1980s-era archetype into a modern guise is exactly what prompted *Vogue Paris*, the zenith of Chaix's childhood fashion fantasies, to call. The commission in question was a story with photographer Alasdair McLellan for the October 2009 'Supermodels' issue, featuring iconic 1980s supermodel Claudia Schiffer. 'I was thrilled to get a call from Emmanuelle Alt because she and Carine Roitfeld had worked for the magazines I was looking at in my teenage years: *20 Ans*, French *Glamour*, *French Elle*,' explains Chaix. 'My country and my culture will always be very important to me. Even if I've been living abroad for most of my adult life I still feel very passionately about France.'

Her intense passion and unique skill for melding the strands of different narratives into a tangible, believable story did not go unnoticed by Proenza Schouler, for whom Chaix has been collaborating since the Spring/Summer 09 collection. Chaix works with them on each collection from its inception – from researching ideas to creating new silhouettes, from the show to the advertising campaigns. 'Marie's unbridled passion for the work she does is contagious,' offer Hernandez and McCollough. 'She is an endless cauldron of ideas. Being around her for just a brief second is enough to inspire us and get us moving in a new direction. We need a feminine perspective in what we do, and have found that voice in her.'

As is often the mark of a true original, however, where the ideas that shape that voice come from is more difficult to pin down than the result. 'My inspiration? Everything and nothing,' says Chaix. 'It can be how someone tucks their jacket into their jeans walking down the street, images I love or simply a piece of art.'

Marie Chaix

Pages 58–59

Ultra stylized, dynamic glamour of the kind that has become Chaix's trademark. Photographed by Richard Burbridge for the Spring/Summer 2010 issue of *Self Service*.

LEITH · CLARK

When Toronto-born London-based stylist Leith Clark launched *Lula* magazine in 2005, she instantly became the frontwoman for a new breed of femininity in fashion imagery. As an outlet for Clark's personal take on the world at large, the magazine unleashed a refreshing homage to romance and beauty, while, as a template for style, it brought modernity and credibility to an almost invisible dialect of girlish charm. It was Clark's ode to fashion, to women, and has made her a significant figure in international fashion.

Starting her career as an intern for *Interview* magazine in New York, Clark came to London in 2000 to assist (her heroine) Kate Phelan, fashion director at British *Vogue*. It was there that she honed her innate taste for the fairy-tale wonderland that high fashion can offer, but a series of much earlier encounters with the power of sartorial fantasia had already started to forge the nostalgic tics that characterize her own styling.

'The thing that was the biggest influence in the beginning for me was the Childlike Empress in the film *The NeverEnding Story*,' says Clark. 'I remember being this little girl and putting necklaces on my head and seeing the way that transforms you. I was an only child, under the table at the dinner party alone, playing with imaginary friends and then, all of a sudden, you put a ballet costume on me and I wasn't afraid to perform. That's when I started to learn about the power of clothes.'

Resolutely playful and tightly bound to that same idea of fashion as a clear-cut conduit for fantasy, *Lula* inadvertently redefined the perimeters of independent magazines on its launch. 'It wasn't something I ever anticipated doing so it was very primal and instinctual,' admits Clark. 'We worked on the first issue as if it was the only one.' Hosting a million girlish fantasies, its candy-coloured art direction, whimsical photo shoots with an easy, almost conversational delivery of high fashion, short stories and interviews with female icons as disparate as Dolly Parton and Zooey Deschanel, presented an enchanting antidote to the prevalence of fierce fashion in the majority of European style magazines at the time.

A combination of secret diary and girls' club fanzine, but with the production values of a high-end glossy (a legacy direct from the creators' premier fashion schooling – the magazine's original creative director Becky Smith was also ex-*Vogue*), *Lula* fast became a compendium of female crushes. An affirmation of the power of fashion as both a liberating and also a celebratory force, *Lula*'s tagline 'girl of my dreams' summarizes Clark's view of the magazine as a celebration of women and of individuals. It also deliberately conjured up the importance of integrating dreams into the midst of daily life, suggesting that literally nothing is out of reach. Nor are notions such as playfulness and success mutually exclusive. 'For me, we have a very feminist approach in a way,' says Clark. 'We're women writing and creating for women. You're allowed to not grow up and you're allowed to be a strong woman all at the same time.'

Lula is a vista into Clark's universe and, as such, delivers a journal of inspiration for its audience while also being a reflection of their tastes. A constant, yet unpredictable flow of unusual yet often high-profile women (actress Kirsten Dunst guest-edited issue 5, while Kate and Laura Mulleavy, the duo behind fashion label Rodarte, co-edited issue 11) has been a key factor in keeping the magazine's legion of loyal global followers hooked and also helping retain its cult status.

Clark's aim with *Lula*, as with everything she does, is to keep the dream in motion. Exposing the grubby underside of real life has no place in the fantasy package that Clark, along with her team of creative collaborators (photographer and publisher Damon Heath, writer Charlotte Saunders

Bodysuit, Topshop. Shoes, C.
Olympia. Hat, Suzanne Couture M.

and film-maker and trapeze artist Sarah Sophie Flicker), freely admits she creates for herself. 'I made *Lula* for myself, I still do,' says Clark. 'And to reveal the guts to the world is just not the point. I don't want to know. I just want to have the dream – whether that be a realistic one or not.'

With the magazine now safely out of its infancy, it has established her as something of a figurehead for fashion romantics, the poster girl for an aesthetic that travels with her in both her editorial and commercial work. Her list of additional work includes contributing fashion editor for a host of international *Vogue*s; print, television and film campaigns for Chanel; consultancies for Cacharel and Orla Kiely; and an enduring professional relationship with actress Keira Knightley.

Such is the genius of *Lula*'s widespread success and Clark's unique interpretation of what women want, that even the name has become a byword for girlish cool for a number of high-street brands. '"Lula" even seems to have become this weird adjective,' says Clark. 'I was with the team from Topshop the other day and they said to me, "listen we have this project happening and it's very "Lula".'

While Clark's distinctive visual language is based on channelling a specific brand of naïve charm, she is under no illusion of just how powerful a tool that can be or the impact it has already made. 'With fashion, I think you can kind of trick yourself into feeling how you want to feel,' suggests Clark. 'It's not about money – it's about magic. A dress really can make the world for a day.'

Leith Clark

Page 64

A series of *Lula* covers. Clockwise from top left: Model Siri Tollerod for issue 6, Spring/Summer 2008, photographed by Ellen Von Unwerth; the Lolita-inspired issue 2, Spring/Summer 2006, photographed by Damon Heath; issue 12, Spring/Summer 2011, photographed by Damon Heath; Kirsten Dunst at the helm of issue 5, Autumn/Winter 2007, photographed by Karen Collins.

ANNA · DELLO · RUSSO

'There are two types of people in fashion: people who work in fashion and people who are obsessed with fashion,' says Anna Dello Russo, the inimitable editor-at-large and creative consultant for Japanese *Vogue*, a woman for whom the latter is indisputably the case. One of the most photographed fashion editors of all time (by the time the Paris shows are drawing to a close she is already starting to plan her wardrobe for the next set), Dello Russo has a curator-like, fanatical appreciation of artistry and an ability to throw her dynamic visual imagination into any situation, making her one of fashion's most covetable forces.

Her chameleonic character shifts, powered by fearlessly tackling some of the wildest fashion looks known to woman on a daily basis, have sealed her highly blurred personal/professional mythology. Born in Bari, a wealthy area of southern Italy, Dello Russo knows a world that has always been typified by a sense of extravagance. Like a magpie, attracted by fashion's shiny things, she recalls learning to cherish beauty from early on, a desire to wear couture from the age of twelve and how, as a dyslexic child who struggled with language, she quickly found an ally in fashion. It was a medium within which she could express herself with an innate ease: 'I was born with a fashion imagination,' says Dello Russo, 'always looking for fashion in other parts of my life.'

Dello Russo is now the stuff of fashion folklore, but the media fascination that currently has its focus tightly trained on what outfit she is wearing belies the fact that her accomplishments span decades. Her pantheon of supporters stems from her rich back catalogue of fashion stories, authored in collaboration with some of the world's most iconic photographers, past and present – Helmut Newton, Bob Richardson, Steven Klein, Mert Alas and Marcus Piggott – which were created during her rise through the echelons of *Vogue Italia*.

She is well known for her extreme glamour and powerful sense of decadence that harks back to her youth in Bari, but it is actually a keen sense of drama that underscores everything she does. One of Dello Russo's favourite stories is a black-and-white Helmut Newton shoot for *Vogue Italia* in 1996 in which model Carolyn Murphy, dressed in men's tailoring and with tightly cropped blonde hair, stands on the edge of a cliff holding the blindfolded young model Jaime Rishar. 'It's about a fascination with the dark side of life, being on the rocks of life,' explains Dello Russo. Another image, also taken by Newton, but this time a portrait of Dello Russo herself, shows her with her hair pulled back, striding through a Milanese piazza in a long black coat and men's shoes. Barely recognizable as the Anna Dello Russo of the front rows we see now, it perfectly epitomizes the way in which she uses fashion to craft character and shift from one personality trait to another.

Having studied art history in Milan, Dello Russo completed an MA in fashion (under the tutorship of, among others, Gianfranco Ferré), before becoming an accessories editor at *Vogue*. By 1989, she had been spotted by legendary editor-in-chief of *Vogue Italia*, Franca Sozzani. It was a period that she describes as being, 'The basis for everything I am now.'

In 2000, she detoured into the world of men's fashion, becoming editor-in-chief of *L'Uomo Vogue*. 'It was a good challenge and an important moment in my life but I also found it a little claustrophobic,' says Dello Russo of the impressive six-year stint, admitting that her love of the comparative flamboyancy of women's fashion was her true calling. In 2006 she made a celebrated return, taking her current role as editor-at-large of Japanese *Vogue*.

In addition, her position as creative consultant to several major fashion houses, none of whom she will name for fear of jeopardizing the intimate relationships she has come to cherish, continues to mark Dello Russo as a figure of great relevance. Much like the late Isabella Blow, as an industry figurehead, her personal mythology is partly derived from the fact that she is living proof of high fashion being able to exist beyond the perceived inaccessibility of the catwalk; but what also makes Dello Russo so valuable is a lesser publicized but extremely acute self-awareness. Her public image is both utterly intentional and completely authentic, an expression of her personal mantra that fashion is essentially about 'adding colour and joy to every situation'.

'There is a lightness in fashion,' says Dello Russo, 'a superficiality, which it is good to carry too. It is inside – you just have to find it. Fashion is not just something you can wear – essentially it provides a sense of yourself. The creative process is a way of dreaming and that's why I always push women to play with fashion.'

What is also special about Dello Russo, and comes as a legacy of her considerable time in the highly pressured job of magazine editor, is that she has kept her relevance at a premium by embracing the generation of fashion bloggers and sartorial chroniclers who follow her every move. Her own blog, which she works on religiously every evening, has achieved cult status among the fiercely contended fashion blogosphere. 'Before blogging, advertising revenue was about the biggest feedback you could rely on, but that was truly just a business voice,' explains Dello Russo. 'The Internet means that you can at least understand how the new generation see you. It's given me the energy to feel like a beginner, to engage again like I did at the very beginning.' Proof of its reach lies in the fact that when Lanvin's artistic director, Alber Elbaz, collaborated on a range with H&M, one of the first places the collection was sent for a publicity call was Dello Russo's flat, and a shoot (starring Anna) was produced especially for her blog.

Dello Russo also appeared wearing a daring gold Balmain dress on the cover of the special tenth-anniversary edition of *10* magazine, published in Winter 2010, affirming the rare affection in which she is held by both fashion fans and the industry elite. Even more extraordinary was the launch of her perfume, Beyond, for Christmas 2010: a Cinderella-style glittery gold bottle in the shape of a shoe, which has made her the first fashion editor to have broken into cosmetics, confirming just how far the previously invisible world of styling has come.

So, what is the secret to Dello Russo's almost iconic fashion status? Expressed with an affection that holds palpably spiritual undertones, apparently it is complete and utter dedication. 'Fashion is a process, not a thought, that requires humility and devotion – a constant curiosity,' says Dello Russo. 'You want to learn English, then fall in love with an Englishman. It's the same with fashion – be around it and you will be able to speak it in all languages.'

UE 37
nter 2010
ce £6.95

10

LET'S CELE BRATE

MARKUS EBNER

Markus Ebner

Page 75

The cover of *Achtung*,
issue 11, Spring/Summer
2008, photographed by
key contributor Gregor
Hohenberg. The issue
showcases Ebner's
fashion-fantasy-meets-
real-life approach
to styling.

While pragmatic creative sounds like a contradiction in terms, it is an apt assessment of stylist and editor-in-chief Markus Ebner, whose straight-to-the-point, fashion-meets-life approach to style has made his magazine, *Achtung*, a vital cultural touchstone for a new generation of Germans.

Ebner studied at the Fashion Institute of Technology in New York, but learned what he calls 'the real language of fashion' at legendary PR and production agency KCD in New York, before moving to menswear magazine *Details* as fashion director in 2000. In 2003, living back in Germany and frustrated with the prevalence of cultural references that he saw being borrowed from the USA and UK, Ebner launched (without any commercial backing) the independent biannual fashion magazine *Achtung*.

Meaning 'attention' or, more accurately in this context, 'watch out!', *Achtung* swiftly became a visual fashion-based anthology in homage to a generation of German creatives united in their pursuit of wanting to affect a fresh, original and crucially modern perception of Germany. 'When I moved to Berlin from New York I got to know a group of young photographers who were all looking to create an image of the new Germany, and I knew I wanted to be involved as well. I like to work with other people who have an understanding of history and an ambition to have a voice and a place in history.'

Ebner's strategy rejected the obvious icons of German fashion (and potentially the easier route to acclaim) on the basis that those who had achieved superstar status abroad were too far removed from Germany to connect with the new wave of creativity he was aiming to rouse into life. 'I didn't want to rely on the established German photographers like Peter Lindbergh or Ellen Von Unwerth,' explains Ebner, 'because it's too well-known a visual language, too stereotypical. *Achtung* was always about developing a new platform to represent a new generation of tastemakers.'

The aim was to create what Ebner describes as 'an icon of chic', something definitively German and a product that would travel but, above all else, would remain forever synonymous with its true cultural origins. 'I want people to take *Achtung* back from Germany the same way they take Pastis from Paris,' declares Ebner.

Looking for allies, Ebner, almost accidentally, found one of his strongest in the art photographer Walter Pfeiffer. As a pioneer of realistic imagery in the 1970s and an artist whose pictures of hedonistic, free-spirited youth have been cited as an influence on some of Germany's most directional fashion photographers, such as Juergen Teller, Pfeiffer was an ideal match for Ebner. They met via an interview for *Achtung*, when Pfeiffer had been in self-imposed photographic exile for almost a decade, and realized that they had an immediate affinity. His was a low-key world of minimally styled beautiful people that Ebner also had his eye on.

'Before that I'd never dared to shoot for magazines because I felt it was just too mediocre,' explains Pfeiffer of his fear that shooting for anything outside a pure artistic context would force him to dilute his creative vision. 'But my private and public images are the same when I work with Markus. It's always fun and that's the point. Right now everybody wants something, like never before, whereas he gave me the strength to move into something new. Before Markus I just did it for myself.'

Despite acknowledging a love of fashion as 'something that can make you dream', Ebner is emphatic that *Achtung* is concerned with the reality of fashion and is not fantasy driven in any way. The coarse paper and the hands-on approach (every piece of content is commissioned from scratch) indicate the raw, home-grown foundations essential to its propagation as a countercultural style bible.

But the significance falls further than a renegade aesthetic. Ebner's creation, sold predominantly in Germany, Austria and Switzerland and by request in the USA and Japan (a deliberately small distribution to keep the magazine covetable), not only charts the personal evolution of a creative from stylist to editor-in-chief but also identifies a generation in transition. A generation still wishing to exorcize the powerful stigma of guilt attached to the abstract notion of national identity. 'We are a generation finally with nothing to apologize for. The idea [with *Achtung*] was to present an idea of a stylish German allure by working with people of a certain generation,' he asserts.

Ebner is also editor of *Sepp*, a biennial title that mixes football and fashion. As the forerunner to *Achtung*, it is a magazine to which he credits *Achtung*'s existence – '*Sepp* taught me to trust my instincts and shape my own visual world' – and an additional platform that he believes connects with heterosexual men who struggle to make sense of high fashion's general bias towards 'super-sexualized or ambiguous imagery'.

'I like being a men's stylist who offers a counterpoint to the very stylized imagery out there,' says Ebner. 'When I'm casting, I'm always looking for an interesting young man who has a good personal look to develop a story with, and I very often let the model interact with my clothing rack so that he can pick what he wants to make the photo look accessible and real. To show men in fashion without them looking like slaves to fashion is very dear to me as it's a field that leaves much room for improvement.'

Entirely comfortable with leaping into unknown territories, Ebner plans to shift his attentions on to a new project in the near future, launching a magazine that fuses fashion and food. 'I think great fashion designers and great chefs are very similar in the way they source and create' – but it is clear that fashion will always play a pivotal role in the mechanics of his unique creativity. As Ebner says, 'Everyone wants to be in fashion – or fashionable.' For visionaries such as Ebner, there is no better way to change the world.

Markus Ebner

Page 78
Footballer Hidetoshi Nakata, photographed by Jork Weismann for issue 3 of *Sepp* magazine, Summer 2006.

Page 79
A series of *Achtung* covers. Clockwise from top left: Issue 14, 2009, photographed by Jork Weismann; issue 10, 2008, featuring model Barbara Berger, photographed by Markus Jans; issue 7, 2006, photographed by Jork Weismann; model Toni Garrn, issue 6, 2010, photographed by Walter Pfeiffer.

EU € s CH SFR 9 DE DK 55 SE SEK 75 **2009**

ACHTUNG

ZEITSCHRIFT FÜR MODE

EU: € 8,00 GR: SFH 14,00 DK: DK 65,00 SE: SEK 80,00 NR. 10|2008

ACHTUNG

ZEITSCHRIFT FÜR MODE

Paris, Paris

ANNA HEIDEGGER „À POIL"
EXKLUSIV FÜR ACHTUNG VON
JORK WEISMANN IN PARIS VOR DER
YVES SAINT LAURENT BOUTIQUE
AM PLACE ST. SULPICE FOTOGRAFIERT

SARA BERGER IN CHANEL BIKINI VON MARKUS JANS EXKLUSIV FÜR ACHTUNG IN MEANS FOTOGRAFIERT

ACHTUNG

4 196272 405004 16

ZEITSCHRIFT FÜR MODE

D: € 8.00 A: € 9.00 CH: SFR 14.00 NR.07|200

ACHTUNG

ZEITSCHRIFT ✠ *für Mode*

in Hamburg in Versace

FAMILIENBANDE

'Katy has incredible energy and vision. She draws her inspiration not just from fashion but also from history, music, media, literature and film. It has always been an incredible experience creating images with her,' declares fashion photographer Mario Sorrenti on connecting with England's talent. Such is the exceptional level of reverence applied to England, a stylist whose reputation as a consummate creative force has been instrumental in transforming the perception of her profession from a playground for muses who flirt with inspiration to a groundbreaking arena for world-class visual innovators.

Indeed, to watch England at work is to witness fashion's sublime capacity for reinvention. Constantly immersed in a phoenix-like process of deconstruction and regeneration, devising new items from the carcasses of others, England produces work that hinges on the notion of creation rather than translation. Her early fashion training at Manchester Polytechnic was, according to England, a practical rather than creative course based on 'pattern cutting and industry', but has proved to be the perfect anchor for her creativity. Few items, looks or ideas remain untouched in England's hands, every one better for her instinctually conceived, perfectly executed interventions. Playing with traditional etiquette is the very essence of England's methodology. 'It comes down to process for me. I often enjoy the process more than the end result, and mixing it up is exactly what I'm about. I don't even think I've ever worn one look in my entire life. Even Alexander McQueen was at a push. I have to personalize everything,' confesses England.

Her acute grasp of the fundamental skills of fashion design has punctuated England's career at many critical moments, including one of her (and the industry's) most seminal professional relationships: her partnership with the late fashion designer Alexander McQueen. As a creative marriage of epic proportions, even the story of their meeting follows a script laced with pseudo-romanticism. After noticing each other at the Paris shows, McQueen approached England in London and asked her, in quintessential British style, to have a cup of tea with him 'because he wanted me to style his show'. A bond was instantly formed. 'I said, "I don't really know what to do or how to do it but I'll help you." And that was it, we hooked up,' explains England. 'We felt like we were invincible – like we could do anything together.'

He was the *enfant terrible* of British fashion, whose sublime skill and vision would charm the notoriously impenetrable Parisian ateliers. She was the hard-working rebel stylist and co-visionary who became his ultimate creative accomplice. According to photographer, and long-term ally of both artists, Nick Knight, the pairing was both magnetic and unstoppable. 'Katy brings a rock-and-roll factor to what she does – that kind of mix of energy, darkness and sexualized sensuality. But there's also a flirtation with death, very much like there is with rock-and-roll bands in fact – a fascination with the very fine line between life and death that can enable some people to feel more alive. Lee's work was incredibly dark so it's no coincidence that they worked together.'

England headed up McQueen's London design studio, but when the designer took up residency at Givenchy in Paris, England went too, leaving behind her directorship of style bible *Dazed & Confused* (a role she later reprised in part, assisting publisher Jefferson Hack to set up *AnOther Magazine*) to assume the role of creative director. 'I was there as a designer with him,' recounts England. 'It was the whole process – from researching to being at every single fitting with him, from realizing and commercializing a collection to directing shoe and bag designers.'

Katy England

Page 80
A Nick Knight image from the seminal 'Fashion-able?' issue of *Dazed & Confused*, September 2008. Guest edited by the late designer Alexander McQueen, the issue challenged conventional perceptions of beauty.

Alongside other creatives such as art director and set designer Simon Costin, England and McQueen cultivated a world pinioned on an intense round of shows, that allowed McQueen's vision to soar beyond anything the fashion industry had ever witnessed before. Fashion shows became large-scale productions, legendary experiences that galvanized the entire industry. A new touchpaper had been lit that exposed fashion's conceptual underpinnings in all their glory.

England cites two shows as enduring favourites: the seminal Givenchy couture show in 1998 – forever legendary for its inclusion of celebrated double amputee and paralympian Aimee Mullins striding down the catwalk in a pair of bespoke prosthetic wooden legs; and 'Robots', the Spring/Summer '99 show that culminated in model Shalom Harlow's layered white dress being sprayed by giant robotic arms.

With Mullins featured on the front cover of *Dazed & Confused* at the same time, it offered up fashion as a potential agent for social change for the first time in decades. Beyond the spectacle, it was a direct challenge to contemporary definitions of physical beauty from the unlikeliest of sources. 'It was a very personal moment,' says England. 'It was more than a fashion show. It was my duty to show something else – an idea way beyond fashion. One of the models said to me, "I never thought I could look so beautiful" and that was it for me.'

The stylist's appointment as creative consultant for the phenomenally successful Kate Moss collection for UK retailer Topshop is further evidence of her full grasp of the design process. Echoing the multifaceted nature of her earlier roles with McQueen, the collaborative role at Topshop – swinging between stylistic instinct and design direction – has spanned fourteen seasons and has further cemented her mercurial prowess.

'Working with Katy on Topshop was so easy as she really understood how to translate my ideas without letting them become too distracted,' says Moss. 'Katy has a unique way of making clothes her own, she will always be re-sewing, adding layers or sometimes stripping off excess to make a certain point of view. She always brings a genuine aspect of street style or that really cool factor to a character or the mood of the girl in the story.'

It is this mix – her rare ability to navigate the push and pull of couture and mainstream, design and styling, editorial innovation and commercial magic – that has provided her with not only an enduring career but also an unrelenting edge. England's star is as bright and as current as ever. How does she retain that position? Apparently – despite working with many of fashion's most coveted and fantastical image-makers, including Nick Knight, Mert Alas and Marcus Piggott, Inez and Vinoodh, David Sims, Annie Leibovitz and Steven Klein – it is by keeping it real.

'In all honesty, I probably always look to the street before the catwalk,' suggests England. 'I generally go for real people rather than models because, for me, it's about how somebody wears the clothes and how it becomes really personal. I've done plenty of crazy fantasy stuff of course but my preference is to veer towards reality. I'm just drawn to it. Ultimately, I guess it's a realness for me that I've always got to have in the picture.'

EDW
ARD·
ENN
INFU

Pages 88–89

Enninful's visual dexterity is at full strength for this story for the October 2008 issue of *i-D*. Photographed by Emma Summerton.

Since achieving the, still unsurpassed, accolade of being the youngest ever fashion editor (aged eighteen) of an international fashion magazine (*i-D*), Edward Enninful has shown extraordinarily deft dual mastery of both street style and haute couture, often simultaneously gracing the same image. It has made him one of styling's most dominant forces and the ultimate aesthete.

Instantly recognizable for their sublime combination of grace, poise and ultra-modernity, Enninful's images, whether on the pages of *L'Uomo Vogue*, Italian or US *Vogue*, a Lanvin billboard or the iconic winking portraiture of *i-D*, have an inherent vitality that delivers a subtle but precise impact. Tracing that vitality back to its roots, Ghanaian-born Enninful's initiation into fashion came via what has become one of fashion's greatest fairy tales involving fellow stylist Simon Foxton, who spotted him – aged sixteen – on a train on his way to college. A stint modelling for Foxton and legendary fashion photographer Nick Knight followed, as did his submersion into the seductive cultural bricolage that was *i-D*. It wasn't long before Enninful, who had grown up in the multicultural maelstrom of Ladbroke Grove in West London, started giving Knight direction on how he thought he should look. Drawing inspiration from the layers of rich visual references by which he had been surrounded, he swiftly dispensed with modelling in favour of creating stories of his own devising.

'Before I started modelling or working for *i-D*, I would always draw and sketch. I was obsessed with female soul/R&B/disco singers growing up,' recalls Enninful. 'I would collect their records and obsess over the way they looked – I'd re-sketch them and draw the singer in lots of new outfits. Also, my mother was a dressmaker. I would work with her in her studio, sketching and helping to dress the women who came in for fittings. So, there was always an element of creativity and fashion in my life but I never wanted to be a designer. It wasn't the construction of a garment I would be thinking of. It was more how a person can change with fashion and the stories that can be told.'

As one of a group of key innovators that broke through in the mid-1990s by flouting conventional fashion etiquette, Enninful creates images that have been instrumental in reinventing street style. A clear progression from the early days of *i-D*'s much-imitated straight-ups (now echoed by every fashion-based photo-blogger), they also challenge the illusion of good taste. So graceful is Enninful in adding a spiked edge to sophistication or a street-style influence to high glamour that, despite his images always having the appearance of being tailored to perfection, closer inspection reveals that the impact often comes from a perfect set of contradictions: pitting restraint against vulgarity, scavenged Portobello market finds against haute couture or humour against the backdrop of high fashion's super-serious lavish façade.

Whether it is Lily Donaldson, as captured by Emma Summerton, sprawled across a series of sky-blue diner banquettes wearing Christopher Kane lace minidresses, or the pseudo-goth beauty captivating middle America in Steven Meisel's 'Modern Magpie' editorial, it is the artfulness of Enninful's styling that provides the ultimate validation. Nothing is impenetrable under Enninful's watch, the end result always both seductive and intriguing. When translated into a commercial arena, it has become an immensely valuable Midas touch for Enninful, who has worked on campaigns for Lanvin, Christian Dior, Dolce & Gabbana, Armani and Calvin Klein (to name just five). He makes any collection not just palatable but deliciously enticing.

Having actively pursued the casting of edgier young models, such as Devon Aoki, Kristen McMenamy and fellow Londoner Kate Moss in his early days, Enninful's portrayal of interesting characters based on a hybrid of carefully cultivated references has been of phenomenal significance.

'I think it's just from being honest with my styling,' declares Enninful. 'I have never strayed too far with who my woman is. She is essentially one person – it's just her situation that changes. My woman is a cross-bred species that has elements of Ladbroke Grove, Portobello, grunge, Kate Moss, Brigitte Bardot, Helmut Lang, the 1960s, Buffalo, Fellini, Italian/ French new-wave cinema, military and my mother. She's a real melting pot of inspirations.'

Though many of Enninful's extensive portfolio of *i-D* covers show barely a scrap of clothing, the attitude, hair and make-up all signal Enninful's presence, a vivid articulation of just how far the stylist's role as image-maker pushes beyond the clothes themselves. A true cover veteran, Enninful had a defining moment (and indeed so did the fashion industry) with the launch of *Vogue Italia*'s August 2008 'Black' issue, an unprecedented issue populated entirely by black models. Masterminded by editor-in-chief Franca Sozzani in league with Enninful, the acclaimed issue directly challenged the industry's deficit of black talent and served as an industry-wide call out to casting directors, editors and advertisers by showcasing not only established superstars such as Naomi Campbell, Iman, Veronica Webb and the young Jourdan Dunn but also a wealth of up-and-coming models. 'That was an amazing issue and an honour to be part of,' recounts Enninful. 'As a black stylist, I personally feel it is very important to continue to push forward. I am aware that the number of black people working in the industry is limited and the "Black" issue did open people's eyes but there is still work to be done.'

Still young by industry (any industry) standards, Enninful continues to seduce, surprise and push boundaries, no matter which brand, collection or magazine he is working on. 'Some of the most old-school people in the industry will comment on a story I've done in *i-D* and the fashion kids love *Vogue Italia*, so the arena's boundaries have blurred, it's one big theatre really.'

Edward Enninful

Page 92
From Giorgio Armani's Spring/Summer 2010 advertising campaign, photographed by Josh Olins. Armani is just one of several major fashion houses to have eagerly embraced Enninful's sublime creative ingenuity.

Page 93
A series of *i-D* covers. Clockwise from top left: Jessica Stam in a beauty special for the September 2004 cover, photographed by Richard Burbridge; Kate Moss for November 2007, photographed by Emma Summerton; Kristen McMenamy photographed by Juergen Teller for March 1996's 'Alternative' issue; the February 1992 issue, photographed by Simon Martin.

NICOLA FORMICHETTI

Nicola Formichetti

Pages 94–95
A typical Formichetti-
style high-energy spread
from the story 'Tribes'.
Photographed by
Sølve Sundsbø for the
Spring 2007 issue of
V Magazine.

Nicola Formichetti is a fashion-fuelled visual-communications icon for the YouTube generation: a stylist, director, designer and curator whose infectious energy and progressive work ethic have shunted the smouldering romance between fashion, music and magazines into a brighter, more hotly debated, spotlight than ever before.

Creative collaborator-in-chief to pop sensation Lady Gaga, creative director of luxury French fashion label Thierry Mugler and contributing fashion editor to a host of magazines including *V Magazine* and *V Man*, *Dazed & Confused* and *Vogue Hommes* Japan, Formichetti is constantly flexing his creative muscles. He describes fashion as 'being at its best when it's totally of the moment'.

Formichetti moved from Rome to London in 1997 on the pretence of studying architecture, but his true education came courtesy of London's club scene, which introduced him to a thriving editorial subculture led by such magazines as *Dazed & Confused, i-D* and *The Face*, who were inextricably pinned to the uncensored, experimental medium of street fashion. It was while partying that Formichetti met many of the characters that were to shape his vision, including Yuko Yabiku, with whom he started the legendary independent boutique The Pineal Eye (originally conceived as a Japanese toy store). As the first store in London to stock avant-garde designers such as Bernhard Willhelm, Viktor & Rolf and Jeremy Scott, it became a hub for London's most progressive fashion editors, including Katy England and Alister Mackie of *Dazed & Confused*, who offered him a solo spot in the magazine, in honour of the store, called 'Eye Spy'.

Two years later, in 2004, publisher Jefferson Hack offered Formichetti (then twenty-seven and having never assisted another stylist) fashion directorship of *Dazed & Confused*. It was a vital, high-profile turning point and a role that forged seminal partnerships with photographers and designers including Steven Klein, Hedi Slimane and Nick Knight.

Formichetti's reputation grew steadily courtesy of his fearless, uninhibited disregard for boundaries, and remains characterized by an unpredictable, experimental edge and an easy understanding of the power of hybrid combinations – a direct legacy of his Italian and Japanese heritage. 'I was mixing Japanese streetwear with Italian high fashion. It was all about contrast. I was putting women's clothes on men, and men's clothes on women. It was boys and girls and androgyny and really fucking everything up.'

The same infectious energy and innate sense of fun has reverberated with enough force to attract a large number of commercial clients including Levi's, Alexander McQueen's diffusion line McQ and Dolce & Gabbana – a role Formichetti actually reprised after a disastrous early collaboration, while still getting to grips with the commercial side of the industry. 'I had no idea what I was doing,' recalls Formichetti. 'I thought I'd done the most amazing job. I thought my total fearlessness was brilliant. I got sacked the next day.' He is now also the official fashion director for Japanese high-street fashion brand Uniqlo.

It is Formichetti's incendiary collaboration with Lady Gaga, however, a woman whom he believes transcends the traditional concept of celebrity, that has become his most significant creative relationship to date. The pair first met on a shoot in Miami for *V Magazine* after he had persuaded editor-in-chief Stephen Gan that they should shoot the then unknown singer. The story runs that she turned up – already in full make-up, hair and dress – and blew Formichetti away. The chemistry kicked in instantly and the galvanizing alliance of fashion and music was sealed in significant style.

96

The two now work as reciprocal muses, with Gaga referring to Formichetti as 'fashion's freedom – my friend, my genius, my collaborator', and have created outfits that are already the stuff of fashion legend. The white lace 'cocoon' outfit for the 2010 Brit Awards (an impromptu last-minute switch, conceived as an unspoken homage to the late fashion designer Alexander McQueen); the controversial 'meat' dress worn to the 2010 MTV Video Music Awards in Los Angeles; and a host of equally outré line-ups for videos such as 'Bad Romance', which featured a white gimp-style latex suit and razor-blade sunglasses, have arguably made her the most important fashion-propelled pop fantasy since Madonna.

'Until I met her it was all about fantasy and creating something surreal,' says Formichetti. 'In a way it feels more powerful with her [than simply styling for an editorial shoot] because it's real. We turn up and we create. For me she's not a celebrity. She's a performance artist.' Having orchestrated the fashion for the videos for 'Bad Romance', 'Telephone' and 'Alejandro', Formichetti has made the transition into moving images, which presents another inspired phase in his pioneering career and even greater visual presence in the virtual world he has grown to adore.

A creature of modernity who claims to be 'over magazines', because 'they're just too slow', Formichetti is hungry to communicate his work quickly and as widely as possible. 'I want to use technology to change the way the whole industry operates,' he declares. He is constantly attuned to his own blog, twitter feed and participating in live screenings of projects for photographer Nick Knight's interactive platform SHOWstudio.

When his inaugural menswear collection for Thierry Mugler hit the catwalks in January 2011, Formichetti confirmed his commitment to taking creativity online by devising an exclusive, Web-only film (featuring tattooed model Rico Genest) to follow the show. With Gaga acting as music director for the project, choosing the show/film as the vehicle to unleash a brand-new bespoke track, all Formichetti's favourite worlds collided in the most satisfying way possible.

According to Knight, Formichetti is 'one of the few stylists who has really engaged with the Internet as a way of using fashion,' making him its current ruling force. He also suggests that Formichetti's embrace of the hyperreality of the online world was an obvious choice for someone who has worked a radical vision of fashion from the beginning. 'What you're always looking at with Nicola is a remix of influences that he throws back to you in a sort of stunning cocktail. He has such a desire to forge into the future with images that seem so extreme you'd think people wouldn't necessarily engage, but they do,' says Knight. 'The Internet is now the primary vehicle for fashion and Nicola is leading that.'

Continuing to redefine the concept of what it means to be a stylist, a creative director or whatever may come next, as a supreme DIY creative Formichetti epitomizes the notion that (paraphrasing what fellow stylist and mentor Katy England once told him): if you believe in what you are doing in fashion, there are no rules that cannot be broken when you are prepared to explore, connect and embrace the world around you. 'Maybe this is where I start fucking with fashion,' he concludes. 'Magic really happens when it's all connected. Fashion, art, music: culture.'

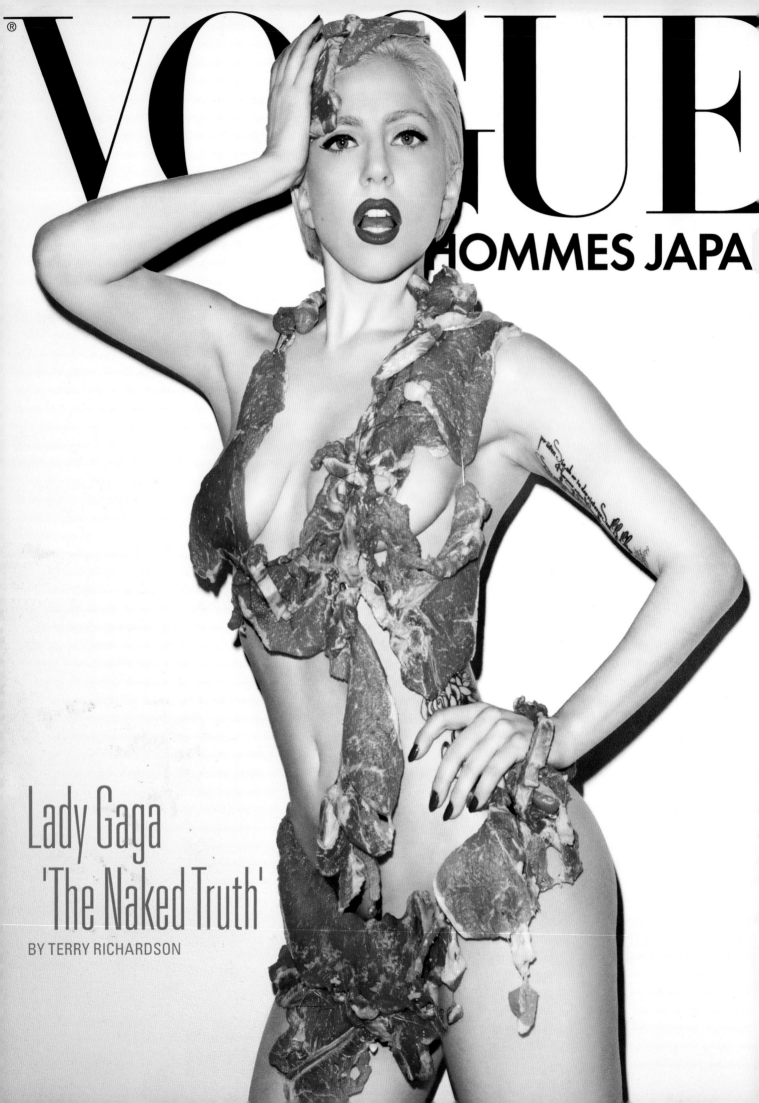

VOGUE

HOMMES JAPA

Lady Gaga
'The Naked Truth'

BY TERRY RICHARDSON

SIM
ON
FO
N
T
X
ON

To look over the vast landscape of portrait-based imagery that comprises Simon Foxton's career is to witness a trailblazing trajectory of the shifting depictions of both menswear and masculinity, spanning more than twenty-five years.

From his own post-graduation fashion label Bazooka, created in 1983, to becoming editor and, later, fashion director of legendary style magazine *i-D*, via numerous brand consultancies and artistic accolades, Foxton has a unique and colourful language that remains a benchmark for all those involved in the art of styling. An infallible ability to tether symbolism and fantasy, teased from all areas of modern culture, to the syntax of contemporary fashion, makes him one of the most significant stylists in the industry.

It was Foxton's time at Central Saint Martins College of Art & Design in the early 1980s, alongside other members of fashion's burgeoning vanguard such as designer John Galliano and art director Stephen Male, that set his innovative pace. The college was at the epicentre of London's incendiary club scene, and Foxton's most formative fashion education came, by default, from clubs The Blitz and Hell and the potent sexual energy of the emerging gay scene. 'I remember that we had to get in at 9.30am to sign the register, and there were people turning up in completely blue make-up and full-length wolf-skin coats,' remarks Foxton. 'The college itself was like an extension of the clubs, that's where everything was really happening.'

The line of Foxton's distinct vision can still be traced back to those days, when his creative trademark of provocative, fantastical subversion – underscored by a subtle wit – first took hold. It was a universe of wild new possibilities, a cartoon-like dreamscape of fashion fuelled by sex (and vice versa), which Foxton plugged directly into. 'My shoots are really my dream world,' he explains. 'That's how I'd like people to be. And, in a way, that's how I want to be. I think that most of my shoots are really like some kind of therapy, what I'm trying to do is create what I want to be.' Photographer Jason Evans, one of Foxton's most seminal collaborators (alongside photographer Alasdair McLellan and Nick Knight, with whom Foxton first emerged into the spotlight) affirms this: 'Working with Simon, I often find myself visually transported to another world, to his world. It's life as he'd like to see it, creating possibilities and celebrating the experiential.'

Foxton's work, whether it is a playful subversion of machismo or a response to shifting cultural boundaries, always entertains as well as informs. Images from the *Arena Homme Plus* story entitled 'Galliano's Warriors', photographed by Nick Knight in 2007, show Foxton playing with greased-up, minotaur-head-wearing models in a feral display of super-sexualized, hyper-masculinity; while 'Strictly' by Jason Evans for *i-D* in 1991 – a shoot depicting formally styled black men in suburban settings – tampers with traditional English house-and-home-style portraiture in an exploration of heritage, ethnicity and the metamorphoses of modern culture.

'He has a deep passion for black culture and he's always expressed it in a way that is light-hearted and intelligent,' reflects Knight, who worked as a team with Foxton, almost exclusively, throughout the 1980s. It was a time when Foxton's work was at its boldest, brightest and tightly bound to a stream of Afro-Caribbean influences. 'A lot of Simon's work followed in the tradition of R&B album covers that have this incredible energy, but what he creates isn't from an alienating or threatening perspective. It's almost like he's taken that world and re-contextualized it within the English countryside.'

Simon Foxton

Page 105
From the 'Strictly' story, photographed by Jason Evans for the July 1991 issue of *i-D*.

Page 106
Examples of Foxton's often radical, always insightful, depictions of men, three of which were showcased at the retrospective of his work, 'When You're a Boy', held at The Photographers' Gallery, London, in 2009 (excluding top right). Clockwise from top left: A powerful example of Foxton's portraiture published in the February 2009 issue of *i-D*, photographed by Ben Dunbar-Brunton; from *i-D*'s May 2010 issue, photographed by Karim Sadli; a key image from 'Punk', for the February 1986 issue of *The Face*; from the story, 'I Wish I had Invented Blue Jeans', photographed by Simon Thiselton for the August 2008 issue of *i-D*.

Uniquely for a stylist and courtesy of his longevity, the body of Foxton's work has unintentionally come to be viewed as a retrospective visual anthology of male identity, represented not only in magazines and fashion advertising but also within established bastions of British high culture, including Tate Modern and the Victoria & Albert Museum. The show 'When You're a Boy' at The Photographers' Gallery, London, in 2009 confirmed Foxton's status as a stylist whose skill transcends any previous professional perimeters. Curated by London College of Fashion lecturer and editor-in-chief of *The Gentlewoman* Penny Martin, it is the first exhibition of imagery that a stylist, rather than a photographer, has headlined as the creative lead.

The artistic synergy illustrates the extent to which Foxton's genius comes from a passion for image-making and storytelling that surpasses the need to grasp fleeting fashion trends. For Foxton, it will always be the larger issue of communication that gets his creative juices flowing most spectacularly. 'It is of course a hugely important industry, which I've been a part of for a long time but, in some ways, fashion as a concept jars slightly with my way of thinking,' says Foxton. 'I use the building blocks of fashion, the clothes and accessories, as tools for my pictures, but I'm really not too bothered about whoever is doing what this season, that's not how I come at it.'

Ironically, it is exactly this innate ability to construct powerful fashion imagery, images that have a longer-lasting resonance and can dig brands a firm place in the consumer psyche (beyond the threshold of a single season), which has endeared him to fashion labels such as Levi's, Caterpillar and Stone Island. His creative process, which involves devouring thousands of images (from magazines, the Internet, films) before he appropriates them in a new guise, has helped to establish an original core identity for many brands whose evolutionary path requires them to be both in synergy with fashion and also able to survive beyond its fickle backlash. It was indeed with Levi's, with whom Foxton's role as stylist often slipped into the adjoining remit of creative direction, that Foxton first commissioned the then fledgling photographic talents of contemporary industry powerhouses such as David Sims and Craig McDean.

Foxton remains one of the most influential and progressive stylists working today. Now co-director of the creative fashion consultancy &Son, which he founded with fellow stylist Nick Griffiths, Foxton is yet again using his powers as a cultural curator to refresh and redevelop a fresh legion of new brands. Playing on the vast patchwork of skills attained during his phenomenal career, &Son tackles every aspect of brand language from fashion design to campaign strategy, from photographic commissioning to, of course, styling.

'When you get it right it's very exciting and satisfying because it's the culmination of all the research, the ideas, the talking, the production,' attests Foxton. 'It's an incredible thing to discover that suddenly you've created this new type of being.' What is the next stage in the evolution of Foxton's beings? According to the artist, a menswear collection for older men.

KATIE

·GR

·GR

AND

LOVE

THE ANDROGYNY ISSUE

THIS IS HARD CORE

LEA AND KATE PHOTOGRAPHED BY
MERT ALAS AND MARCUS PIGGOTT

When issue one of *Love* magazine struck in February 2009, having racked up more anticipatory hype than any other fashion-based title in history, it still managed to exceed all expectation. Featuring on its cover singer Beth Ditto in all her supersize, naked glory, it redefined the parameters of mainstream magazine publishing and confirmed its editor, Katie Grand, as one of the most significant and fearless game-changers in fashion.

Covering more ground than possibly any other stylist in the world, Grand is many things to many people: stylist, consultant, editor, art director as well as curator. What you see in the collections she has styled for Topshop Unique, Giles, Ungaro, Prada, Miu Miu, Loewe and Louis Vuitton, the magazines she has contributed to (*Interview*, *Industrie*, Russian and Japanese *Vogue*) and those she has launched (*Dazed & Confused*, *AnOther Magazine*, *Pop*, *Love*) is not only a formidable talent for nailing the moment, but also an unshakeable belief in her own instincts (no matter how much they go against the grain), which has propelled her into fashion's visionary elite.

To prove the point, nothing Grand does follows a formula. Even her attendance at Central Saint Martins College of Art & Design – the recognized incubator for most top European fashion talent – does not come with the standard story of broadening horizons or having helped her find creative solace. Grand describes Central Saint Martins as something of a comedown. 'I'd been this golden girl, a star pupil and then when I got to Saint Martins they were having none of it. They were more into people who were cutting off mice's heads and making prints out of their blood. I wasn't weird enough, and they weren't interested.'

More concerned with the real world than fashion theory, in 1993 Grand got the education she had really wanted alongside fellow innovators publisher Jefferson Hack and photographer Rankin with whom, in the role of fashion director, she created *Dazed & Confused* magazine. What began as a student style fanzine became one of Europe's most respected independent magazines and gave Grand an appetite for mixing fashion and pop culture.

It was while at *Dazed & Confused* in 1994 that Grand got the call to style Kylie Minogue for *Top of the Pops*. It was a moment that Grand confesses was one of the biggest thrills yet. 'It was my first real experience of a famous person,' she recalls. 'And it was something that made a difference in the real world, which really mattered to me.' In 1999, she applied that insight to *The Face* as fashion director, tailed closely in 2000 by an offer to head up *Pop* magazine, a lavishly produced 'superglossy', which meshed celebrity and fashion in a braver, bolder, more liberated (and fun) way than ever before.

Featuring attention-grabbing covers of female stars from all corners of celebrity, including Madonna, Kate Moss, Sienna Miller, Drew Barrymore and Kylie, it was high-end style but also had a brilliantly cartoon-like, tongue-in-cheek cool. When Grand put a portrait of Victoria Beckham on the cover, with the tagline 'oh darling', she handed her a new credibility. Like most of her cover stars, they have remained friends ever since. 'Katie has an incredible energy that translates into everything she touches – both personally and professionally,' says Beckham. 'She has never been one to feel the need to conform, she simply follows her instinct and heart.'

Groundbreaking imagery and the ability to always remain true to a personal vision, no matter how high the stakes, also define Grand. She describes the launch of *Love*, which incorporated both, as one of the defining moments of her career. 'When Nicholas Coleridge [managing director of Condé Nast, UK] saw the image he said, "Are you sure?" And

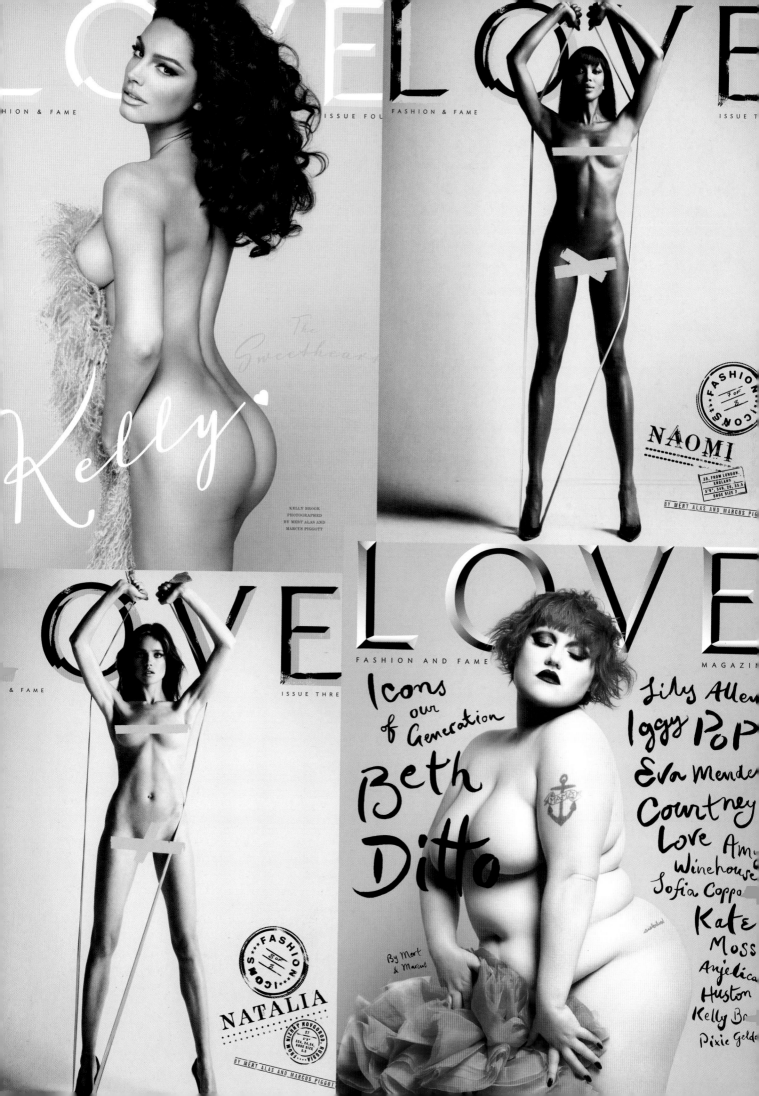

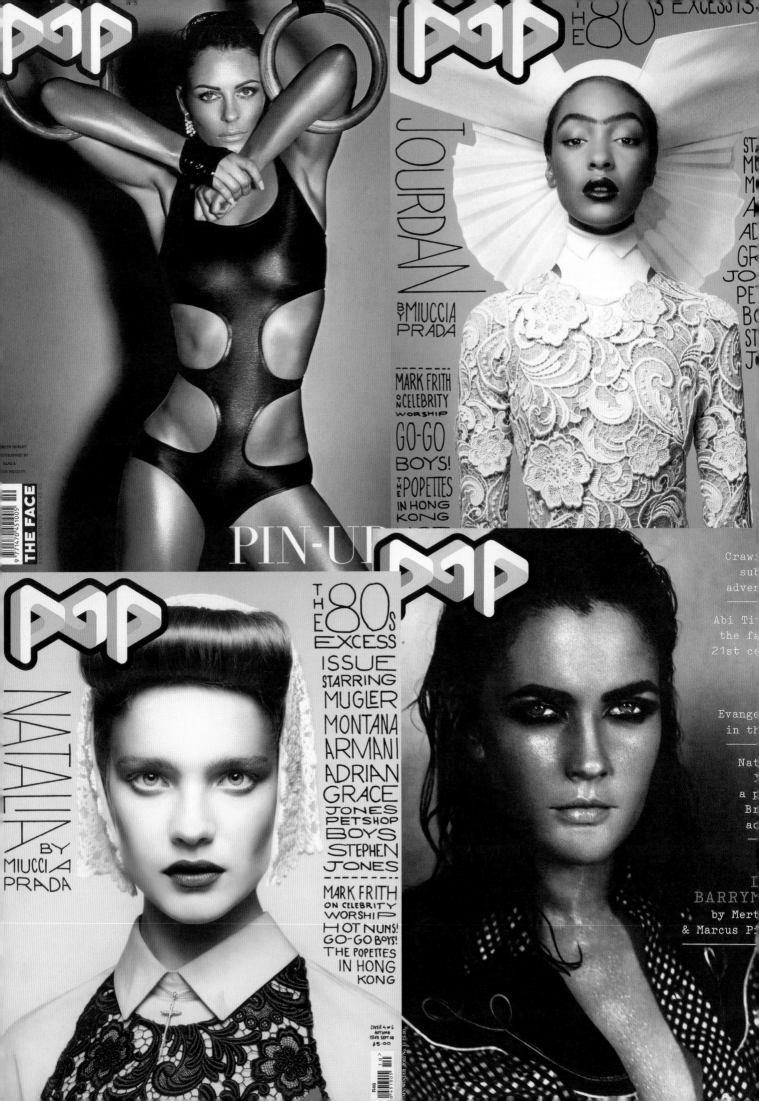

I said that I'd never been more sure in my life.' Grand was aware of the controversy it would generate, that of course being exactly the point. 'The worst thing is when people don't even notice, which is why I tend to veer toward sensationalism – especially on magazine covers,' she confesses.

Grand's bravado and her acute understanding of the value of creating a strong brand hook had been honed via the publishing industry but it was also being formed, simultaneously, during a series of consultancies for major fashion houses. It started with Bottega Veneta in 1998, which she describes as having been 'a major crash course in work', carried on to Miu Miu and then Prada. Prada's 'Sex' show for Autumn/Winter 02/03 is another of Grand's most memorable moments. Grand's input played a significant part in redressing the critics who had accused Miuccia Prada of being incapable of making sexy clothes, and shone a new spotlight on the label previously revered purely for its classicism. 'Before that show Prada had never really been about sex – and they never really were after it either. It felt very different. It was a monumental show,' recalls Grand.

Of all Grand's creative relationships, the most visible, however, is with designer Marc Jacobs, with whom she is in contact on a daily basis, often discussing ideas via text as diverse as the proportion of a jacket to the entire theme for a new collection. 'We're kindred spirits in that we have this simple love of clothes and getting dressed and although she may hate this I can actually see her as a kind of alter ego in a way,' declares Jacobs.

It is also her humour that apparently keeps him buoyant. Jacobs explains, 'We share the same sort of perversity, or irony. There's a level of boredom and amusement at the same time, which is important because to be entertained shows some kind of conviction. But that's not to say she isn't focused – she's also extremely thorough and attentive. I think that since we started working together the collection has been better than ever.'

Grand's ability to whip legions of new ideas into being, while never compromising on the detail, is legendary (with *Love*, she infamously checks every line and Cromalin repeatedly before production) and proof of Jacobs' assertion that Grand was built for the constant revolution of fashion. When asked whether there are any influences to which she constantly returns, she half jokes that, 'if you can work out what someone was into when they were thirteen then that's what they'll always be into'; and 'when I sit down to do anything there's always a bit of David Byrne, Nick Rhodes, Neil Tennant, Prince, Kim Basinger in the film *9 ½ Weeks* and [most powerfully] Melanie Griffith in *Working Girl* in what I do.' Where those influences manifest themselves, however, is more difficult to second guess, and what makes Grand grand.

'Just like when you're working on a collection, you know that when you start the next issue it will be a complete reaction against everything we did last season, which I'm aware, of course, isn't always the most commercially viable idea, but that's what you do. It's like with the music industry, everyone wants you to do the same album, they don't like it when you change, but that's the nature of fashion. Then again, when you look at David Bowie...'

Katie Grand

Page 116
A selection of covers from Grand's 'superglossy' *Pop* magazine. Top left: Actress Elizabeth Hurley for the Autumn/Winter 2002 issue, photographed by Mert Alas & Marcus Piggott. Top right and bottom left: Supermodels Jourdan Dunn and Natalia Vodianova for the '80s Excess' issue, Autumn/Winter 2008, photographed by Sebastian Faena. Bottom right: Hollywood actress Drew Barrymore for the Autumn/Winter 2005 issue, photographed by Mert Alas & Marcus Piggott.

Pages 118–119
Grand's tribute to luxury fashion label Louis Vuitton, using historical pieces from the brand's archives to celebrate the opening of its first 'Maison' in London. Photographed by David Hughes.

JACOB
.
K

Jacob K

Pages 120–121

From 'A White Story', featured in the April 2010 issue of *Vogue Italia*. The image displays the deeply poetic, otherworldly sensibility that underpins Kjeldgaard's styling. Photographed by Paolo Roversi.

Page 122

Another example of Kjeldgaard's often intense styling, photographed by Josh Olins for *Vogue China*, November 2008.

Page 123

From the 'High-Style' shoot, photographed by Tim Walker for *Vogue Italia*, September 2010.

'Fashion is about moving people. If you aren't moved or entertained by what you see then it's not right,' declares Jacob Kjeldgaard. The Danish-born stylist's bewitching, otherworldly aesthetic and intuitive approach to crafting strong, poetically charged fashion imagery has already established him internationally as one of the most masterful new storytellers in fashion.

Leaving rural Denmark in 2001, Kjeldgaard moved to London to work with designer Peter Jensen as a studio assistant. His immersion into fashion's editorial hall of excellence was as swift as it is impressive. He swapped Jensen's design studio for London's vibrant magazine culture, working as an assistant to stylists Anna Cockburn and Olivier Rizzo. His first solo work – a series of menswear stories for editorial heavyweight *L'Uomo Vogue* in 2003 – marked an unprecedented debut and a preternatural kink in the conventional order of progression. Created in tandem with one of his most significant ongoing collaborators, photographer Tim Walker, the stories showed the maturity of Kjeldgaard's perspective and flipped established convention, which decreed that young stylists should spend years toiling at independent magazines before breaking the international scene, on its head.

Kjeldgaard's natural charm and modest self-assurance flourished, delivering the formula-deflecting niche that still keeps him tantalizingly just beyond the tethers of fashion's often fiercely tribe-like communities without having to abandon them altogether. Trading on his allure as a professional free spirit, Kjeldgaard now walks regularly among the holy grail of glossy fashion titles, such as *Vogue Italia*, *V Magazine* and *W* magazine, while also being invited to shoot with a host of revered style titles such as *i-D* and *Dazed & Confused*. He has also styled shows for design houses as diverse as Cerruti, Burberry Prorsum and long-time collaborator Richard Nicoll, who describes Kjeldgaard as having a 'rare calmness and a genuine charm that completely informs the way he works'.

'Usually it does go the other way around and you find people from your generation, you build up something and you grow together,' says Kjeldgaard. 'For me, I found that having already started working with a very established photographer early on, I had to move the other way, and find people later, but in a way it made me quite free. Different magazines allow you to do different things. I'm using those different outlets to express the different things that I want to say, but that fact that I'm not really considered part of one specific magazine means you can't really pin me down.'

That sense of illusiveness has indeed developed, if not as a blueprint by which his work can be distilled, then certainly as the core of his distinctive creative bias. Toying with issues central to the fashion machine – what is considered contemporary, what is obsolete – Kjeldgaard has a penchant for fantastical worlds, either spun from a surreal, Alice in Wonderland-esque thread or from an era-defying reportage-style approach. Both have more in common with the intuitive, mood-establishing visuals of cinema than they do in demonstrating fashion trends, not to mention a crucial exchange between perceptions of good and bad taste. It is in skirting around the edges of vulgarity, moving dangerously close to the verges of territories lesser stylists would not dare to touch, that Kjeldgaard appears to have found both his creative nirvana and his inimitable signature.

'I think I try really hard to find that balance because I always say that it's really easy to do quite a cool fashion photograph, but doing that whole thing where you're playing with elements – elements that, for example, could ultimately be very sugary and twee – is a lot harder,' he explains.

124

Kjeldgaard's collaborators insist, however, that a razor-sharp understanding of fashion's relevance is never far away. 'For me, as a photographer, I rotate around my world, specifically my childhood and I need people around me who can break into that bubble and hold a mirror to me in a way that tells me what's relevant,' states Tim Walker. 'If it were left to me my work would look like a Mr Kipling advert. He [Kjeldgaard] injects a relevance to the spirit of the time and he's very strong with it. He has a rod of steel when it comes to fashion and will force me to do things that I otherwise wouldn't.'

Characterization is also an essential part of Kjeldgaard's work, with every shoot meticulously constructed, whether it is a Walker-led, large-scale, high-colour visual extravaganza complete with ball gowns and set builds, or a one-model, black-and-white studio shoot with photographer Paolo Roversi. 'He has an innate understanding, a respect for women and is versatile in his ability to do modern pared-down chic as well as highly theatrical layering and everything in between,' attests Nicoll, with whom Kjeldgaard has been forging looks for six years. 'He has a passion for defining the character for the shoot or show and illustrating her idiosyncrasies; like him, his work is very human.'

Never overpowering but always powerful, that sense of humanity and a belief in the art of styling as a collaborative discipline are what has imprinted Kjeldgaard's personal stamp on the image-making process. On every occasion, it is the characters that form his central contribution to the final visual platter.

'I think I'm more intuitive than intellectual in my approach to styling,' he insists. 'I'm very sensitive to everyone who I'm together with within that creative process, whether it's the character I'm trying to portray or the photographer I'm trying to engage with. With the characters, quite often it's a character that I'd like to hang out with or who might make me laugh. Or someone who is so outrageous...it doesn't have to be a good thing, it can also be a really bad character, someone who you're really intrigued by.'

Ever the beguiling outsider, less concerned with following protocol than he is with continuing to plough his own creative furrow, for now Kjeldgaard is content to 'take it as it comes', striving to perfect the skills he has developed with the relatively small but elite group of photographers (Tim Walker, Paolo Roversi, Benjamin Huseby and Sarah Moon) with whom he has been honing his craft since the beginning. 'I think that you're only as good as your last shoot and every shoot is like a new discovery,' states Kjeldgaard. 'It's sensational when you get in front of the camera and you get all your tricks out – you almost get quite high from it somehow.'

Jacob K

Page 126
Kjeldgaard brings his ethereal touch to a Spring/Summer 2009 shoot (featuring model Stella Tennant) for luxury brand Hermes' magazine, *Le Monde d'Hermes*. Photographed by Tim Walker.

Page 127
From the aptly named 'Magic World' story, photographed by Tim Walker for *Vogue Italia*, January 2008.

ALISTER MACKIE

Alister Mackie

Pages 128–129

From the 'Body Language' story, art directed by LucyandBart (Lucy McRae and Bart Hess) and photographed by Nick Knight for *AnOther Magazine*, Autumn/Winter 2010. The image epitomizes the way in which Mackie consistently blurs the boundaries between fashion and art.

Page 131

All forms of artistic endeavour hold a fascination for Mackie, as demonstrated in the dance-fuelled images from the shoot 'Jac & Benjamin', photographed by Nick Knight for the Spring/Summer 2011 issue of *AnOther Magazine*.

The boundaries between fashion and art have always had a blurred midpoint, and in the field of contemporary fashion nobody handles that mutable, fluctuating area better than Alister Mackie. Encapsulating a legion of roles but defying easy categorization, Mackie's career is more accurately appreciated as a series of brilliant creative connections that have stretched fashion to its peripheries and often far beyond.

The common thread and the driving force that runs throughout Mackie's genius is the simple desire to connect, to communicate: from fashion editor at *Dazed & Confused* to directorships of *AnOther Magazine* and *AnOther Man*, from contributing fashion editor at *Vanity Fair* and *L'Uomo Vogue* to an installation for Fendi, a project with artist Sam Taylor-Wood, plus shows, campaigns and creative consultancies for labels such as Marc Jacobs, Alexander McQueen, Missoni, Sonia Rykiel, Dunhill, Lanvin, Louis Vuitton, Topman and Martine Sitbon.

'It goes back to me tearing down pictures and putting them on my wall when I was back in Scotland,' says Mackie. 'To me now, making images, that's the purpose of doing it. More than to sell a shoe or a coat, it's the idea that somebody somewhere needs it [the idea] so much that they're going rip it down and stick it on a wall. Whenever I see whoever it is and they're wearing things from Marc by Marc Jacobs or from Topman it reminds me of that because I still have a sense of being that person in Scotland and I think, inevitably, I always will. That need for information, that need for a visual hit – of somebody communicating something to you.'

Mackie's images are passports to worlds both in and beyond fashion, extraordinary in their boundless appreciation of art, literature, history and film – indeed any expressive cultural medium he can find to appropriate. His love of layering subtexts or introducing an unexpected visual resource (such as painting or sculpture) into the fashion arena is less about subversion, however, than simply about not acknowledging there are rules to break in the first place.

He describes how his initiation into the creative world came from his BA in art (drawing, painting and, finally, textiles) at Glasgow School of Art: 'The first month it was all about making drawings and paintings without even a brush or using paint. In some ways it was a very stiff, old-fashioned place but in other ways it was very freeing. It broke down what you'd thought the rules were...in fact it taught you that there aren't any rules, and I think that's important in terms of the way that I look at creativity. Even today, doing what I do.'

Mackie went on to do an MA in fashion at Central Saint Martins College of Art & Design, but it is principally those art-school habits that continue to pervade his imagery and he is still using scrapbooks to formulate his ideas. Mackie's key creative companion in producing the biannual style magazine *AnOther Man* is an oversized scrapbook in which, every season, he compiles an anthology of research into masculinity, referenced by the team throughout.

'We started off by looking at every which way that men were represented in pictures or painting – all artistic parts of visual culture, except for fashion images – and we now do that every time,' explains Mackie. 'I'm really broad about it. It can be very mass media or it can be very obscure, something pulled up from an art blog. It could be guys in pop videos or it could be something very classic like 1920s photography. Mix it all up, put it into a scrapbook and that's our blueprint.'

Mackie has also led *AnOther Man*'s stories, via the fine-art world, to places where other magazines, before Mackie's lead, would have feared

to tread. Collaborations with artists such as the infamously reclusive Alex Rose, Scott Treleaven, Christian Schoeler and Phil Hale, many of whom Mackie has convinced to take an unprecedented turn behind the camera, have ushered the marriage of fashion and art into new cultural territory, establishing a relevance for both.

'He has a very intelligent vision of fashion, which is very important when you're creating multilayered imagery,' says photographer Nick Knight, one of Mackie's principal collaborators. 'His world is darker, more broken, slightly more poetic than most, but it's not melancholy. He has a love of the bohemian, things that are fragile and delicate and he doesn't try to simplify or resolve things, which is so important. In the tradition of the great painters and poets he relishes things that are complex.'

Back in the commercial world of design and retail, the slippery notion of relevance, of how to maintain pole position at the top of fashion's supremely competitive pile, is something at which Mackie is a grand master. His concurrent consultancies for such omnipresent powerhouses as the luxury fashion ateliers Lanvin and Fendi and the high-street retailer Topman have created an inspirational blueprint for consultancy protocol, demonstrating how to keep each house relevant (in fact at the very zenith of relevance) without compromising on brand identity or values. By applying the same level of impeccable personal taste, coupled with a crucial understanding of the domain, direction and audience that belong to each brand, Mackie has been able to exert an influence with enormous reach. He has also forged a connection between those worlds, previously considered to be entirely mutually exclusive. Whether it is in the cut of a trouser or the hang of a trench coat, the personal inflections that Mackie delivers offer a passage between the fashion-savvy teenager beginning to experiment in Topman and the luxury Lanvin consumer, simply by illuminating the interplay between each.

Working in so many realms and within so many stages of the creative process has given Mackie (who is also rare in his ability to be able to work collaboratively not only with designers but also with other stylists – Katy England at Alexander McQueen and both Venetia Scott and Camille Bidault-Waddington on the Marc by Marc Jacobs line) an astute grasp of the fact that today's high-street fashion enthusiast could be tomorrow's luxury consumer.

To dissect Mackie's genius any more precisely than that is to dispel his creative magic, but what is certain is that what he brings to any shoot, story, brand or collection is a wealth of carefully foraged references designed to add depth to the more frivolous outer layers of fashion. 'He doesn't look for perfection,' affirms Knight. 'He looks way beyond that, which is a gorgeous thing to work with in an image maker.'

Does Mackie himself believe in fashion as a true form of art? 'Yes. And I think it always has been. Just as art has always had a relationship with fashion. They are inextricably linked.'

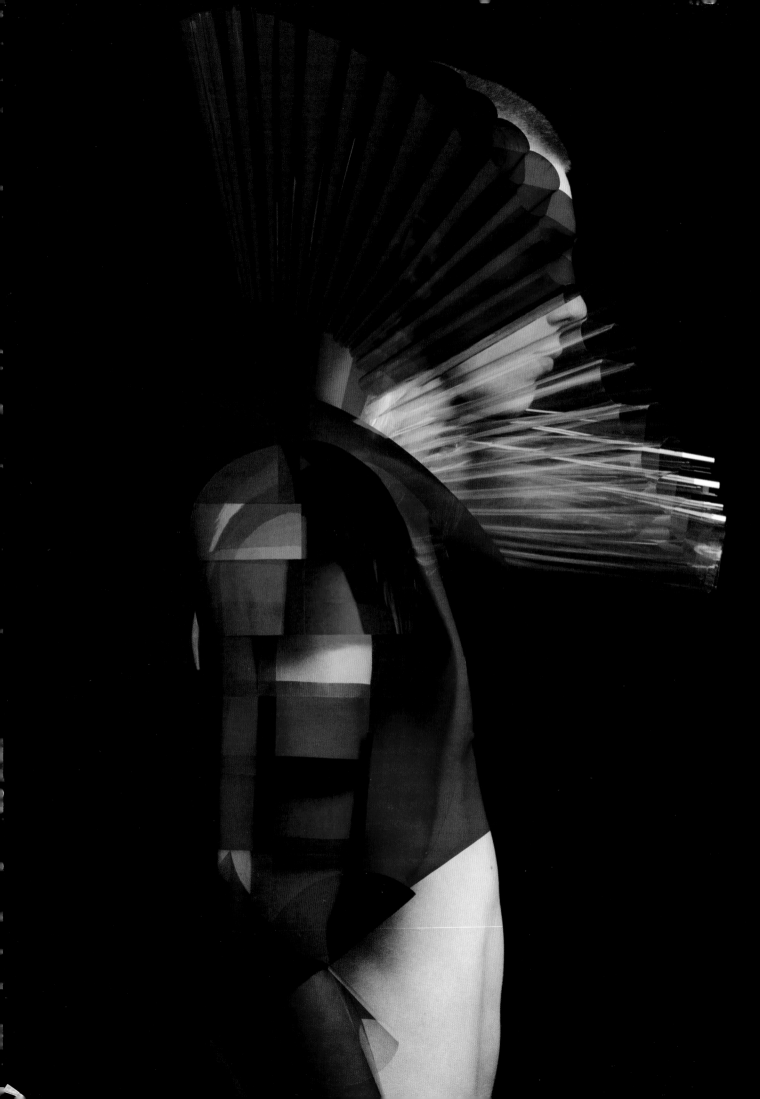

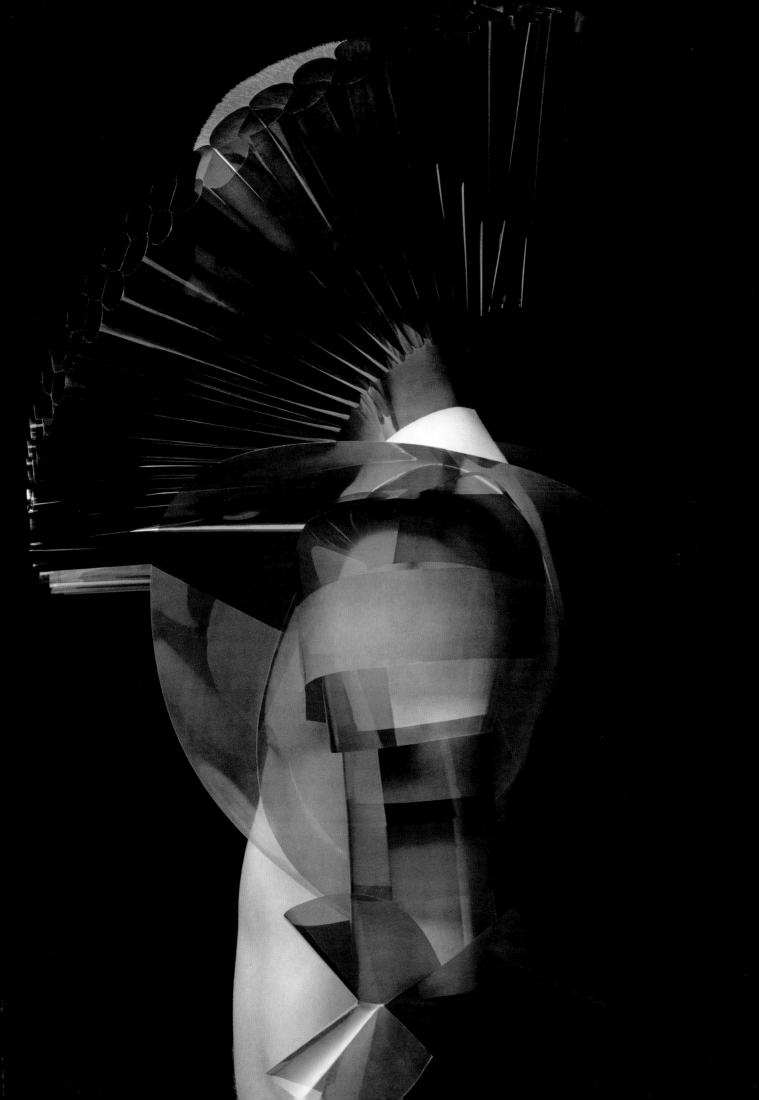

SOPHI
A·NEO
PHiTO
U
-APOS
TOLoU

To be brought into the entrepreneurial orbit of Sophia Neophitou-Apostolou – and it is an orbit, for she has been a seminal collaborative force on a small universe of fashion enterprises – is to experience fashion in the most frenetic and multi-dimensional sense. Often referred to affectionately by designers and other stylists as 'Mama', Neophitou-Apostolou, the hands-on editor-in-chief of *10* magazine (she still styles a significant number of the main fashion stories each season) and *10 Men*, ex-fashion/creative director of *Harper's Bazaar* UK, creative director to designers Antonio Berardi, Roland Mouret and Amanda Wakeley, Elie Saab and most recently collection design director of Victoria's Secret, cuts an inspirational matriarchal figure within the industry.

Powerful women are indeed her thing. Citing *Vogue* power-houses Anna Wintour and Carine Roitfeld, and the iconic former editor of *Harper's Bazaar* US, the late Liz Tilberis, as points of inspiration, Neophitou-Apostolou came relatively late to the industry at twenty-six. Having had what she describes as 'an early mid-life crisis', she re-routed a fledgling career as an interior designer, switching to fashion and the powerful signature style, rooted in a celebration of strong sexy women, that she has maintained ever since.

Moving from work experience at British *Vogue* to fashion director-ships of Russian *Vogue*, *Vogue China*, *The Independent* and *The Sunday Times Style* magazine, Neophitou-Apostolou launched her personal vision of fashion – *10* magazine – in 2000, courtesy of a £15,000 car loan and 'a plastic wallet stuffed with photocopies' of her work. Powering through on sheer self-belief, passion for her craft and an inimitable sense of humour, she created not only a home for her vision of fashion's future but also what she describes as a 'safehouse' for other creatives – predominantly stylists, photographers and writers struggling with the increasingly stringent restraints laid down by commercially backed fashion. 'It affords me [us] freedom, and freedom is a commodity that when you work inside bigger propositions you really understand is the most important thing. It's not homogenized in any way. It's an endorsement of both fantasy and individuality. In *10* magazine, I want them to be the people they really want to be,' says Neophitou-Apostolou.

A legacy of her Greek heritage is the notion of family as a connective and binding force. It is key to Neophitou-Apostolou's methodology, as is her firm belief that an editor-in-chief categorically needs to cultivate honesty, transparency and trust to create the most sublime results. 'I think that sort of level of respect for other people's creativity is absolutely crucial. It's like a tiger you can never really train. There's never a moment you can take it for granted, but once you've understood that you're going to get the result that you want.'

Working in such tight proximity with designers such as Roland Mouret and Antonio Berardi, with both of whom she has forged enduring relationships, Neophitou-Apostolou has been able to affect significant change, injecting her personal vision into the commercial arena. 'You're a sounding board for that person because a lot of the time a lot of designers work in a sort of insular universe. With the shows, you become part of the alchemy of what actually happens eventually, and you get such a buzz from doing those things, as a creative entity.'

Berardi's description of their relationship as 'the story of a marriage' goes some way to explaining how, for him, Neophitou-Apostolou occupies an illusive nexus where inspiration meets insight – a place grounded in intimacy and trust. 'We laugh together, cry together, we argue, contemplate, discuss and console each other,' says Berardi. 'She challenges me

Sophia Neophitou-Apostolou

Page 137
Unequivocally powerful, this image set a creative precedent which continues to define the magazine. From *10* magazine, autumn 2003, photographed by Satoshi Saïkusa.

Pages 138–139
Another iconic image from *10* magazine, Autumn 2003, photographed by Satoshi Saïkusa.

Page 140
A series of images that testify to the 'gritty, sexy glamour' on which Neophitou-Apostolou founded *10*. Clockwise from top: From the Spring 2008 issue, photographed by Cedric Buchet; model Hannelore Knuts, one of the stylist's favourite 'power' models, for the Spring 2005 issue, photographed by Greg Lotus; from the Autumn 2003 issue, photographed by Satoshi Saïkusa; (inset) from the Autumn 2002, issue, also photographed by Saïkusa.

Sophia Neophitou-Apostolou

Page 143
A series of covers
for *10* magazine.
Clockwise from top
left: Hot newcomer Alla
Kostromichova for the
Autumn/Winter 2009
issue, photographed
by Cedric Buchet;
the 'Guerilla' issue,
Spring/Summer 2011,
photographed by Jeff
Burton; supermodel
Karen Elson for
the 'Bitch' issue,
Autumn/Winter 2003,
photographed by Alex
Cayley; iconic model
Angela Lindvall for the
Spring/Summer 2006
issue, photographed by
Alex Cayley.

with every piece: Who is she? Would she wear it? If so, when and where? Is it boring? Is it spectacular enough? She brings the feminine to my masculine, and since the very beginning she has had a profound influence on everything I do.'

Roland Mouret, a designer with whom she enjoys a similarly potent working relationship, has equally high praise for her powers as a conduit of modern femininity. 'She understands the woman I'm dressing so well that she will fight to the end for what she believes is right for that woman,' says Mouret. 'In the beginning, I was adding flourishes to everything and she was the one that told me to simplify, saying "but Roland, women hate flowers, they hate bows!"'

The Galaxy dress, a creation that ricocheted from the catwalk on to every red carpet for months following its launch, epitomizes Neophitou-Apostolou's prowess in using every last detail to help shape his fantasy into a reality coveted by real women. 'She was fighting for that collar to be the link for that whole collection. She told me that I really had to trust her on that, and I did,' says Mouret. 'She is a constant inspiration,' he concludes.

10 magazine, as a rolling documentation of Neophitou-Apostolou's personal creative trajectory, is most noteworthy for its representation of an achingly modern convergence of art and commerce, style and substance. Embracing an unapologetically luxury-oriented stance, it straddles the void between the raw energy of its neighbouring style magazines such as *i-D*, *Dazed & Confused* and *Wonderland*, and the glossy finesse of luxury publications such as *Vogue* and *Harper's Bazaar*. Neophitou-Apostolou herself describes it as 'gritty, sexy, glamour'.

Her shrewd overview of the powerful interplay at work between the worlds of independent image-making, brand illusion and the luxury sector has also meant that Neophitou-Apostolou's style bible has now achieved legendary status as a free-thinking publication, applauded from every angle. Her presentation of high glamour with edge, carried by the womanliest of women, is also indicative of *10*'s agenda as an entirely grown-up vision of fashion – in direct contrast to the fervent celebration of youth culture associated with other style magazines.

By morphing between her roles as instigator, collaborator, muse and master, Neophitou-Apostolou is able to to deliver a recalibration of the codes of contemporary luxury, laying a new blueprint for a contemporary audience hungry for everything that is new and exciting. Embracing every piece of technology at her fingertips, *10* magazine now boasts the 10 blog, 10 TV and its own iPhone application, ensuring that the world according to *10* is always available.

'What we do can afford us gateways to fabulous things and I want to share that. Why wouldn't I?' declares Neophitou-Apostolou of her immense appetite for communication. 'The 10 blog and so on is a whole other universe to express the brand and to talk to other people inside our world [the readers]. I'll be drip-feeding information to my reader until the mother load hits.'

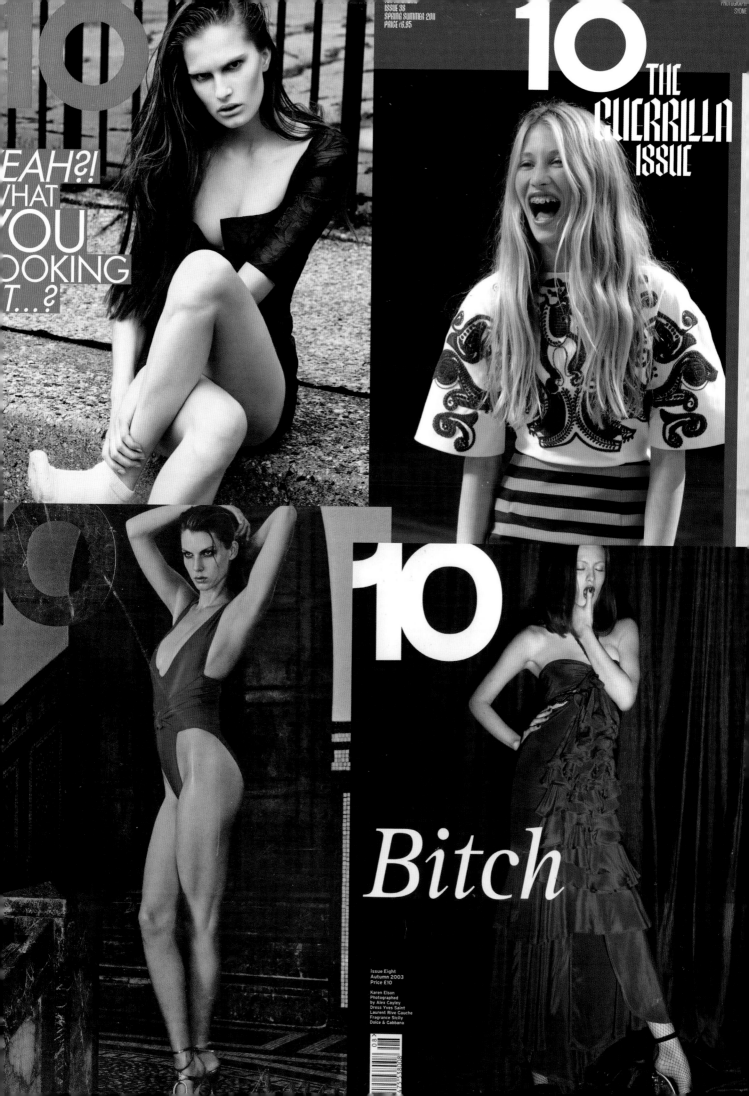

10

ISSUE 38
SPRING SUMMER 2011
Price €6.95

10

THE
GUERRILLA
ISSUE

EAH?!
WHAT
YOU
OOKING
T....?

10

10

Bitch

Issue Eight
Autumn 2003
Price £10

Karen Elson
Photographed
by Alex Cayley
Dress Yves Saint
Laurent Rive Gauche
Fragrance Sicily
Dolce & Gabbana

MAR
IE—AM
ÉLIE•S
AUVÉ

'You must always be the first one to show people the road – you can't look back,' declares Parisian Marie-Amélie Sauvé, in a statement that underscores the visionary perspective on which her career has been built. 'I want to be the one who is still pushing the essence of fashion, because we can't lose that.'

If fashion is inherently driven by the thrill of the new, then the precision-crafted fashion moments co-gifted to us by Sauvé, the progressive ex-fashion director of *Vogue Paris* and seminal figure within the creative atelier of Balenciaga, are essential to its evolution. Less concerned with channelling the current zeitgeist than she is with creating the next, Sauvé is obsessed not only with image-making but also with a level of detail that plunges right down to the core of the clothes themselves, making her one of the most influential stylists of her generation. Her ability to kick-start a trend, whether she is presenting a full shift in silhouette or a severely sculpted shoulder, is infamous, influential and highly in demand.

Sauvé began her career in fashion in the mid-1980s as a nineteen-year-old intern at *Vogue Paris*. It was the middle of a golden era for the magazine, an artistic zenith when its house photographers included such greats as Helmut Newton and Guy Bourdin. Sauvé describes it as both 'her home' and 'the best school to learn fashion', as well as the place that gave her a sense of '*Vogue* the brand', instilling in her an unshakeable understanding of the power of iconic visual communication. Just six months later, she was fully entrenched in one of the world's most influential editorial teams and already crafting a niche for herself via sleek, studio-based editorial imagery authored with photographers such as Newton, Bourdin and, later, Steven Meisel and David Sims.

Renowned for her ability to conjure up an entire world on the back of an architecturally structured outfit, Sauvé explains that the art of great fashion communication involves, 'first, bringing your fashion idea and then creating, with the photographer, a world where you are going to put your styling. I always start with the fashion – never the character,' she insists. 'It's why I love to do studio pictures because when you're in the studio you start with a white page, which is perfect for my strong shapes.'

Sauvé's vision and the crux of not only her editorial genius but also her outstanding commercial value, is anchored in a relentless pursuit of truly original ideas. A self-confessed purist, she rarely attends fashion shows, other than those by a handful of Japanese designers, and believes that 'what is important in fashion is to try not to look at what other people are doing. That's a big fault,' states Sauvé. 'For me, it's very important not to look at other stylists, it's all about my own focus.'

She also describes how she often layers hybrid references to avoid rehashing previous stories or reinforcing easily repeated, already hackneyed fashion narratives. Her personal favourite is a studio shoot for *Vogue Paris*'s September 2007 issue, photographed by David Sims, and featuring model Sasha Pivovarova. She reveals the influences as Japanese designer Junya Watanabe's Autumn/Winter 2007 show and Patrick McMullan's photo diary *SO 80s* – a cultural chronicle of the glamorous, wild and wonderful creatures who defined New York's party scene in the 1980s, including Steven Meisel and model Teri Toye. 'What I'm actually thinking about when I'm working on something is what I could create to give a stronger message. It's more intellectual than real,' declares Sauvé.

The catalyst that took Sauvé's appetite for grass-roots fashion innovation to a new level, however, was when, in 1996, friends introduced her to the then twenty-five-year-old designer Nicolas Ghesquière, recently appointed as head designer at Balenciaga. The chemistry was instant,

Marie-Amélie Sauvé

Pages 148–149

From the Autumn/ Winter 2007 campaign for Balenciaga – a brand that Sauvé's progressive thinking has been integral to for over fifteen years. Photographed by David Sims.

Page 151

Sauvé issues a master-class in futuristic silhouettes via the story 'Une Couture D'Avance'. Photographed by David Sims for *Vogue Paris*, December 2006.

cemented by a shared belief in the fundamental need to present ideas that accelerate fashion beyond the safety net of tried and tested house styles. They have worked together on the Balenciaga brand for almost a decade and a half – a period that has seen the label's kudos skyrocket and its profitability restored. Sauvé's input is interwoven throughout the brand's aesthetic, supporting Ghesquière from the inception of each collection to the styling of both the shows and the advertising campaigns.

She describes their relationship as 'so close it's like family. I have the most amazing memories of being backstage,' says Sauvé, recalling the emotion of the Spring/Summer 02 show. 'The energy backstage was incredible, almost as if we weren't even in the room. And it was really emotional at the time because we were really quite young.' Ghesquière, in turn, describes her with similarly familial affection: 'Marie-Amélie has been by my side for fourteen years. She remains my best friend and my strongest support. Her sharpness and her coolness, along with her knowledge of fashion photography, make her the best fashion editor according to me.'

The work forged by the partnership while Ghesquière has been at the helm of the Balenciaga brand has indeed proved monumentally influential, sweeping through the consciousness of the fashion elite and consumers alike. When the label sent models down the Autumn/Winter 09/10 catwalk wearing sheer black tights with polka dots (something that later figured in the advertising campaign featuring actress Jennifer Connelly), a new trend was whipped into being almost instantly. Similarly, the skeletal black-and-white gladiator boot, from the Spring/Summer 09 collection, gained such coveted status that it spawned a legion of high-street copies despite its low wearability factor.

Echoing Ghesquière's talent for taking elements of the familiar and transporting them to a place that often feels so modern it is practically futuristic, Sauvé explains her methodology as being essentially 'about finding somewhere between a concept and a reality, a place to make your concepts real so that people understand your message.' She explains, 'You are not afraid because of the familiarity, but you are surprised by how that familiarity has been transformed.' In reference to Ghesquière's vision, Sauvé asserts that, 'when you look at the history of fashion, all those big influences – André Courrèges and Pierre Cardin in the 1960s and Rei Kawakubo and Yohji Yamamoto in the 1980s – they were completely new looks and it was a huge revolution. It was a shock, but an intriguing one, and there are very few designers who are doing that now.'

Right now, Sauvé is content to have her hands busy pushing fashion to its limits with US *Vogue*, *Vogue Italia* and *Interview*, a handful of consultancies and, of course, Balenciaga, but what of the long-term future for fashion's most forward-thinking stylist? 'The thing for me with *Vogue Paris*,' muses Sauvé, 'is that it's like my house. I started there when I was nineteen years old, and of course I'm French, so I'm sure that one day I will be back.'

VENETIA·SCOTT

Venetia Scott

Page 153
From *Vogue Italia*,
October 1996,
photographed by the
most significant of
Scott's collaborators to
date, Juergen Teller.

Page 155
Scott's imagery channels
the free-spirited nature
of her subjects in order
to dive below the glossy
artifice of fashion.
Top: Models Hilary
Rhoda and Caroline
Trentini for the 'Future
Will Be Whatever
We Make It' story, for
AnOther Magazine,
Spring/Summer 2007.
Bottom: Lindsey Wixon
for *AnOther Magazine*,
Autumn/Winter 2010.
All images styled
and photographed by
Venetia Scott.

In an industry built on the perpetual motion of shifting trends, Venetia Scott's ability to stand outside fashion's dictates and remain uncompromisingly true to her personal vision is what, conversely, makes her such a valuable creative force. In the many guises she inhabits – stylist, creative director and photographer – Scott is mistress of the quietly powerful, and her ability to burrow beneath fashion's glossy veneer to reveal the enigmatic, raw beauty of her subjects has created one of fashion's most recognizable languages.

As a young teenager, Scott became fascinated by magazines and by the age of eighteen had worked her way into the position of PA to the then editor of British *Vogue*, Beatrix Miller. Swiftly shifting into the fashion team under the directorship of Sophie Hicks and Grace Coddington, Scott was already witness to the machinations of one of fashion's glossiest cavalcades, mesmerized by how closely the reality and the mythology of *Vogue*'s London offices were intertwined. 'It was the whole thing, I guess – the name and that luscious type on the paper, as well as being in an environment with a lot of women who were very inspiring. I simply thought, this is how I want to be,' says Scott.

As Coddington left for Calvin Klein, Scott's youthful infatuation with the bastion of feminine glamour began to fade, however. For a while, she ran photographer Perry Ogden's studio before collaborating with Michel Haddi – the prolific French photographer who was challenging convention by mixing 'real' people (albeit 'real' people graced with a sense of cinematic bravado and an actor's aptitude) into fashion stories. 'He was the first one, for me, who cut out having models and hair and make-up, and we'd often do these trips where we'd cast it once we got there,' she recalls. It is Haddi whom Scott credits for introducing her to an alternative view of fashion, despite their ultimately conflicting views on creative direction. This, in turn, triggered her own, unique take on image-making and a pull away from the populist arena.

Scott's personal understanding of the kind of escapism that fashion can enable and her rebellion against the gleaming artifice she had witnessed at such close range at *Vogue*, was crystallized when, in 1989, she met young German photographer Juergen Teller, and the change of direction was complete. It was in fact Scott who steered Teller into the style that remains his infamous, sometimes controversial, signature. 'She saw the potential in my photographing someone in a way that was very honest and simple,' says Teller. 'At the time I had no idea what fashion photography really meant – she set up a world (with her characters, etc.) that was perfect for me. I essentially helped her visualize the language she already had.'

A poignant indicator of the power of the stylist within the image-making process, Teller believes it was she who rescued him from submersion in a world of mid-1980s fashion imagery obsessed with slick, saturated colours and hyperreality. 'She had an overpowering way...she kind of did overpower me and I don't mean that in a negative way, but she had a very strong sense of what she wanted, which I wanted,' says Teller. An inseparable, irrepressible force for almost a decade, shooting for *The Face*, *Arena* and *i-D* (and later *Vogue Italia*), the Scott/Teller partnership, and their adventures into the unknown, was integral to a style revolution.

Piqued by Scott's fascination with the book *Teenage Lust*, created by the film-maker and chronicler of America's subcultural youth Larry Clark, the pair made an about-turn that revelled in celebrating the raw energy of a vibrant, thriving youth culture. It was a vision of anti-fashion – a potent visual language forged by abandoning hair, make-up and many

MARGARET
HOWELL

MARGARET
HOWELL

of the crutches so synonymous with high fashion – that channelled the fearless, uninhibited spirit of their subjects.

The mystical landscapes of the UK's Cornish coast appear frequently as settings for shoots, as do the wide-open spaces of California. Both provide the perfect settings for the metaphorical freedom that Scott so clearly covets. The boundaries between fashion and reportage have never been so tightly interwoven. Like a film director, Scott constructs fantasy worlds rooted in verisimilitude, and her girls are indeed crucial to the story. Demonstrating her underlying bias toward the character before the fashion, it is often the fantasy girl herself who triggers the idea for a story ('girls who I think I would like to be'), and they tend to fall into two camps.

'I have a tendency to portray two different characters in the images I create,' says Scott. 'One girl has sex in the field – the blonde girl has sex in the field – but the other girl, the dark girl, would be tied down in the bedroom. They are two different characters, but I don't think it's impossible for them to coexist in the same person.' Her comments, which suggest a sense of overlapping agendas – the notion that disparate angles can essentially be forged from the same place – are echoed in the fact that Scott (quite uniquely) also has two different portfolios: one for photography and one for styling. Whether it is her choice of girls or medium of expression, the ideas in Scott's worlds are rarely mutually exclusive.

In 1997, as a result of grunge going mainstream, the call came from designer Marc Jacobs, and Scott consequently became creative director of the Marc by Marc Jacobs range. Her enduring creative relationship with Jacobs (Scott continues to work closely with him) is testament to how she consistently evades the slippery definitions of stylist. Her inadvertently subversive aesthetic – 'I don't have that fearfulness of being categorized because I've never had a strategy' – is as alluring now as ever.

Scott's defiance of limitation was further confirmed by her transition, in 2005, to photographer, a result of her frustration that her images were not being interpreted in the way she had conceived them. Scott has created work for *Purple Fashion Magazine, Self Service, i-D, AnOther Magazine, Pop* and British and Russian *Vogue* (frequently as both stylist and photographer), as well as numerous campaigns for the designer Margaret Howell, and her unique language continues to evolve, amaze and inspire.

'It's important to stay in your own world,' says Scott. 'Leaving time to do nothing is invaluable. I'd much rather stare into space.'

Venetia Scott

Pages 156–157
Two key images from designer Margaret Howell's Autumn/ Winter 2009 campaign, styled and photographed by Venetia Scott.

Page 158
Bearing all the trademarks of Scott's sensual-sexy, retro-modern eye, from a story for *Purple Fashion Magazine*, Autumn/ Winter 2010. Styled and photographed by Venetia Scott.

KATIE

·SHIL

LING

OFRD

Katie Shillingford

Page 161
From 'The Reinvention
of the Supermodel' story,
for the August 2010 issue
of *Dazed & Confused*,
photographed by
artist Roe Ethridge.

Page 163
From the 'Primary'
story, photographed by
Kacper Kasprzyk for
Dazed & Confused's
January 2011 issue.

'If it's not a bit off or doesn't have a twist, I'm not happy. I like to think I have an edge, which allows me to see a beauty in something a bit weird and a bit wrong,' confesses Katie Shillingford, when describing the unique approach to styling that is making her one of the most closely watched stylists of her generation.

As senior fashion editor at *Dazed & Confused* and long-time collaborator with designer Gareth Pugh, Shillingford is central to an influential new generation of trailblazing image-makers (including *Dazed & Confused* accomplice Robbie Spencer) motivated by a bold, experimental vision of fashion. Unconcerned with etiquette, Shillingford does not do normal in any way, shape or form. Hers is a visual language, typified by tangential thinking and an ability to harness the unpredictable in order to create the extraordinary.

Having originally studied graphic design at Camberwell College of Arts, a course that she describes as providing 'a totally free way of thinking' and whose loose perimeters would allow her subsequent shift into fashion, Shillingford quickly became involved with a group of young creatives centred around the !WOWOW! squat in south-east London. Residents included Pugh and the musician/artist Matthew Stone, both of whom remain vital conspiratorial allies within Shillingford's intimate creative sphere. It was via a series of magazine (art department) internships and the beginnings of her partnership with Pugh, however, that Shillingford's talent was recognized by the then fashion director of *Dazed & Confused* Nicola Formichetti, sealing her full transition into the fashion world.

These diffuse creative foundations mean that Shillingford's editorial images often jack-knife between an eclectic mix of references, splicing together a vast library of ideas from the past, the present and Shillingford's take on the future. The fact that her 'Tudor Wench' story, photographed by William Selden for *Dazed & Confused*, was inspired by (but not remotely reminiscent of) a collection belonging to the grand masters of Italian glamour, Dolce & Gabbana, is classic Shillingford. 'It's about taking something, possibly random references, processing them and delivering them with new edge,' she explains.

Pugh describes how Shillingford's ability to spin so many references into one visual entity has had a major impact on his own, inimitable visual language. 'Katie is a great friend as well as a muse and stylist,' says Pugh. 'She's the person who helps meld all of these abstract elements together and is truly an integral part of what I do. I've worked with her from the very beginning, even before my first show at London Fashion Week, where I had her modelling at a show I did at Kashpoint in the club Heaven, trussed up in a black leather pregnancy suit with a long pointy cone strapped to her face. She had to rip away a patch of fabric to unleash a thousand tiny pearls that cascaded from her crotch...we've certainly grown up together, and it's been quite a journey.'

As with many of her predecessors at *Dazed & Confused*, Shillingford's work, whether applied to film, editorial shoots or campaign imagery, is often an exploration of how far the peripheries of fashion can be pushed, bent or transgressed. What is so significant about Shillingford, however, is that her alternative creative logic impacts not only on the high-level, insular utopia of fashion's innovative avant-garde, but also on the mainstream platform of the high street.

While Shillingford has styled the biannual Paris shows for both Pugh and the equally subversive Dutch design duo Viktor & Rolf, her unique touch is as potent within the look books she has created for UK brand

Topshop. Working with what is arguably the UK's most influential fast-fashion retailer, Shillingford occupies a position of immense reach in terms of the vast army of super-savvy, fashion-buying youth, and yet she does not expect the looks she creates to be copied wholesale by consumers. Grounded in a desire to inspire, rather than dictate style in its totality, her skill lies in using fashion to communicate an attitude and incite experimentation. 'I simply like the idea that people shopping at Topshop might be encouraged by me to do something more interesting,' says Shillingford.

Although regularly rooted in fantasy and often heavily accented by an amplified sense of drama (never more so than when with Pugh), Shillingford's theatrics have the unusual quality of being devoid of the schmaltz that plagues other stylists. Bearing fetishistic echoes of the late fashion hero Alexander McQueen, there is an element of extreme beauty to Shillingford's images, an exquisite, often elegant precision – even within her darker, more macabre work – that ensures the resting effect is of intrigue rather than shock.

It is a depth of language unusual for such young talent that, in collaboration with Pugh and film-maker Ruth Hogben, has also helped her craft a niche as one of the leading stylists within the hugely significant fashion film phenomenon. Having fully embraced fashion film, Pugh – assisted by Shillingford – regularly shows his seasonal collections in Paris via film rather than conventional catwalk shows, a medium that Shillingford has also adopted for film projects for photographer Nick Knight's digital platform SHOWstudio. Shillingford describes how, for her, film now consistently outweighs stills. 'Film takes fashion to more people,' she suggests. 'It can give you a more vital energy and a truer understanding of the collection and how it works. I felt like it was a very natural thing to do, especially with Gareth's clothes, it makes total sense when you look at the way they move, blow up – you can see their full form.'

Despite the complex amalgamation of references that form the basis of her work, Shillingford prefers not to fixate too hard on her own internal machinations, insisting that analysis is the enemy of a creative triumph: 'Things are more often unsuccessful when I over-think them. Personally, what I really hate in fashion is things that are too over-styled and too contrived.' When forced to reflect on what it is that makes her equally as alluring to the establishment as to the countercultural ateliers from which she came, she concludes that it can only be the element of wrong that underpins all the rights. 'I do like things to look a bit wrong,' she says, 'but always sophisticated, always beautiful.'

Katie Shillingford

Page 164
Top left and bottom right: From the 'Tudor Wench' story, photographed by William Selden for the November 2009 issue of *Dazed & Confused*. Top right and bottom left: From Shillingford's collaboration with artist Roe Ethridge for *Dazed & Confused*, August 2010.

TAB^I
THA
·SIM
M^NOS

Tabitha Simmons

Pages 166–167

From 'Pure Wonder', a story which showcases Simmons' bent towards ethereal, fantasy-fuelled imagery. Photographed by Craig McDean for the March 2008 issue of *Vogue Italia*.

As brilliantly mercurial as the 'creatures' she divines for the pages of *Vogue Italia*, US *Vogue* and *AnOther Magazine*, Tabitha Simmons – stylist and now also footwear designer – personifies the metamorphosis of stylists from muse to master.

First surfacing on fashion's radar in the late 1990s, as part of the fledgling network of formidable innovators that had begun to emerge from the UK's *Dazed & Confused* magazine, Simmons moved to New York in 1998 to assist stylist Karl Templer. Educated by assisting on the rich variety of Templer's work, absorbing everything from fashion shows to perfume ads, Simmons' ascension onto the global stage consequently came not only with a personal aesthetic, touched by a gothic-inspired beauty, but also with a practicality that asserts her enduring belief that, 'what creates a very good stylist is to be put in any situation and be able to make the utmost of what product you have.' Her inimitable vision has since left an unmistakable imprint on some of the most iconic ateliers, publications and brands in international fashion.

In the space of little over a decade, Simmons has leapt from an early career in modelling (she was scouted while working as a Saturday shop assistant for the fashion label Joseph) to interning then styling for *Dazed & Confused* and *AnOther Magazine*, to the fashion directorship of *V Magazine* in 2002, and consultancies for Calvin Klein, Dolce & Gabbana and Alexander McQueen. She is also contributing fashion editor for both *Vogue Italia*, and, most regularly, US *Vogue*. The addition to her CV of a successful, stand-alone footwear range in 2009 exemplifies just how far the nebulous outlines of the stylists remit can be pushed in the right hands. For while Simmons' career registers the kind of wishlist trajectory that most can only dream of, it has been the irrepressible connection between her wild, fantasy-fuelled imagination and a shrewd understanding of the value of originality that has driven her to the top.

Simmons describes how in her early days on *Dazed & Confused*'s independent ranks, the necessity of working with restricted budgets instilled in her an acute sense of the need for individuality, which has latently fed into her role at one of the world's most commercially savvy fashion titles, US *Vogue*. 'I think that what happened with *Dazed & Confused* has helped me everywhere I've gone because, at the beginning, you wouldn't really get many clothes there so you had to go to the vintage shop, you were forced to create things, to come up with something. There was also no Style.com; we weren't instantly exposed to everything like people are now. By the time you knew what was going on you were doing your own thing by default.'

She describes US *Vogue* 'as a place of extremes', but also as somewhere that has been fundamentally enriching in terms of her development. 'One day you're on the most incredible high and then the next you're in the trenches, feeling like the worst person in the world, but I think that once you've worked there you can work anywhere,' says Simmons. She also credits US *Vogue*'s iconic editor-in-chief Anna Wintour as one of the most significant figures in her career, a crucial supporter. 'She [Wintour] is very good at finding your strengths – whether you want to know them or not. It was there that I properly addressed, "What do I want to say? What's my role here?"'

Wintour is not the only one to have believed in Simmons' creative prowess. Alexander McQueen employed her talents on, among others, two of his most acclaimed shows: the Spring/Summer 05 'Chessboard' show, a theatrically staged visual summation of McQueen's skills; and, again, in Autumn/Winter 08/09 for the spectacular 'The Girl Who Lives in the Tree' collection. The show conjured up the story of a girl emerging from the darkness of a 600-year-old tree – the perfect conceptual match for Simmons' own inclination toward the dark side of fantasy. At the time, many journalists cited the show as one of McQueen's best in fourteen years. It also coincided with the significant announcement that, for the first time, the company had gone into profit.

Dolce & Gabbana also shrewdly enrolled Simmons' styling skills for its Spring/Summer 07 'Sexy Back' show (a fashion house whose shows she continues to style), a sexually pumped, high-energy show that Simmons says she walked out of 'feeling like I was on such a high'. But, Simmons had already begun to nurture a fascination with shoe design. When working as a styling consultant to fashion giant Calvin Klein a few years earlier in 2003, it was on encountering the lasts from which the brand's shoes were created that Simmons started to seriously consider her 'desperate fascination' with shoemaking.

However, it is Jefferson Hack, the entrepreneurial British publisher of *Dazed & Confused* and *AnOther Magazine*, who she credits with orchestrating her final leap from stylist to designer. It was Hack's support, which included securing her a sales representative and delivering practical industry connections (manufacturing and suppliers), as well as calling her every week to convince her of her own talent, that turned her dream into reality.

It is a role she relishes (alongside continuing to style) and a transition that she believes has provided her not only with an exciting new creative platform, but also with an invaluable new perspective on the larger fashion landscape. 'A designer once said to me "Tabitha, your name's not on the door so this is my decision", but now my name is on the door and it is my decision,' she explains. 'But, dealing with that other element, stepping to the other side, has given me a new respect for designers. With styling, it's you – that's it. You can pull in a thousand racks of clothes, but it's you that fingerprints it, who makes that look. But with the shoes there's also the business side, the production side, the sale side – all those things that were a big learning curve for me, I didn't know any of them.'

Every season brings a new wisdom, but the folkloric nuances, a military slant (she cites the 1980s pop phenomenon Adam Ant as well as director Guillermo del Toro's film *Pan's Labyrinth* [2006] as influences) and the antiquated edge that laces Simmons' vein of modernity continue to feed equally in to her designs as they do her styling. 'I'm always into Victoriana and it's always got to have that slightly quirky, feminine side,' says Simmons of her own style. 'And it needs to have that kind of tactile... it has to feel good.'

Whether image- or product-based, Simmons' spin adds a left-field, wholly original beauty that defines her as one of the most exceptional talents in fashion. Wintour confirms: 'She may be incredibly instinctive about fashion, but Tabitha never lets it take her in the obvious direction. It all comes down to the fact that she is British, of course; the place that produced both the most elegant and aristocratic tweedy country dressing and the subversive and anarchic chic of punk. There is a bit of both in Tabitha, and it's the combination of the two that makes her work so very compelling.'

Tabitha Simmons

Page 170
Folklore, Victoriana and military references consistently permeate Simmons' imagery. Clockwise from top left: Fantasy with edge in the story 'The Now Guidelines', photographed by Craig McDean for *Vogue Italia*, September 2009; actress Christina Ricci, photographed by Craig McDean for the Spring/Summer 2007 issue of *AnOther Magazine*; model Stella Tennant, photographed by Craig McDean for the November 2006 issue of *Vogue Italia*; from a story photographed by Willy Vanderperre for the Autumn/Winter 2007 issue of *AnOther Magazine*.

Page 171
A self-portrait of Simmons, photographed by Inez & Vinoodh for the Autumn/Winter 2010 issue of *Love* magazine, for whom Simmons is a contributing fashion editor.

Pages 172–173
Simmons' work for *Vogue Italia* often produces imagery with a darkly fantastical edge, including models that appear to have metamorphosed into mythical creatures. Left: From the 'Theatricals' story, photographed by Mario Sorrenti for the April 2006 issue of *Vogue Italia*. Right: From 'Individual Visions', photographed by Craig McDean for the November 2010 issue of *Vogue Italia*.

FRANCESCO SORIGUES •

Francesco Sourigues

Page 175
Italian supermodel
Mariacarla Boscono
strikes a pose for the
Autumn/Winter 2010
issue of *Hercules*.
Photographed by
Paola Kudacki.

Since 2005, stylist and creative consultant Francesco Sourigues has been responsible for adding a vivacious new accent to the language of men's fashion, significantly rekindling a vision of masculinity that had been on the wane since the 1980s.

Courtesy of his playfully sexy biannual homage to the 'sunnier' side of fashion – *Hercules* magazine – as well as numerous consultancies for a host of influential international brands including Diesel, Loewe, Massimo Dutti and Pepe Jeans, Sourigues has reignited a taste for the outrageously body beautiful. He is the man to go to for menswear styling laced with a brighter, bolder, Mediterranean-influenced edge.

Fascinated by fashion and enthused by magazines from an early age, Argentinean-born, Spanish-based Sourigues describes his route into styling as having come through magazines, which laid out a magical world beyond the parameters of his small hometown. 'I didn't even know that styling existed as such, but I was obsessively collecting magazines,' recalls Sourigues. 'Even travelling four hours by bus to buy international magazines and then travelling the four hours back, the same day. I wanted to do everything from the concept for a shoot to creating that image.'

The move to London in 1999 as a contributing fashion editor for magazines *Arena* and Spanish *GQ* and Spain's leading newspaper *El País*, consolidated styling as the role that would enable Sourigues to fulfil that desire. But, it was the creation of *Hercules*, co-founded with fellow stylist David Vivirido (who had been working with PR agency Purple, while contributing to *The Face*) that anchored his creative ambitions in a solid statement of intent.

Representing a hardcore appreciation of increasingly influential stylistic talent working beyond the epicentres of New York, Paris, London and Milan, Sourigues and Vivirido founded *Hercules* largely based on a desire to salvage a more classical approach to presenting male beauty. After a six-year stint where both had been working for publishing houses in London, in 2006 the pair shipped out to the more exotic climes of Barcelona, delivering issue one of *Hercules* (in October of that year) under the premise of rescuing an aesthetic that they felt had largely taken a battering in the midst of the UK's experimental preoccupation with dismantling archetypal visions of beauty.

'I was no longer identifying with the direction and stereotypes that were appearing in fashion at that time in London,' reflects Sourigues. 'I was looking for a more sunny, healthy, bright and positive vocabulary within fashion and I found it hard to find a place to communicate it.'

Sourigues and Vivirido were not the only ones eager to re-examine the direction in which the contemporary understanding of masculinity was heading (publishing house Condé Nast launched *GQ Style* just a year earlier, under the helm of super-stylist David Bradshaw), but the Sourigues/Vivirido dream was an altogether glossier, more colourful affair tethered to a far more exotic perspective. *Hercules* was always intended as the projection of a full lifestyle fantasy, anchored in fashion and style, but with a specifically – as the mythological-referenced name suggests – Mediterranean perspective. As the antithesis of the London-oriented compulsion to focus the creative lens on reality, *Hercules* was forged as an aspirational world dedicated to beautiful things, gold-standard gorgeous people and, ultimately, living the good life.

Sourigues recalls how he and Vivirido were both fans of the 1980s editions of Italian magazines such as *L'Uomo Vogue* and *Per Lui* (the glossy menswear tome originally directed by *Vogue Italia*'s editor-in-chief Franca Sozzani and which regularly featured shoots by Bruce Weber), whose beautiful and often homoerotically charged imagery made for seductive viewing and an unapologetic appreciation of male beauty. 'We felt it was the right time to go back to that kind of fashion, a more sunny perspective, with the values of classic male beauty,' explains Sourigues.

Proudly rooted in Spain but regularly featuring an astonishing roll-call of international talent, including photographers Paola Kudacki, Daniel Riera and Giampaolo Sgura, stylist Nicola Formichetti and models Raquel Zimmermann and Mariacarla Boscono, *Hercules* has picked up arguably one of the strongest cult followings for an independent magazine to date.

Though undeniably sexy, Sourigues believes that it is the rather more ambiguous notion of sensuality, rather than sexuality, that is the gel that binds one issue to the next. 'Sensuality is crucial for us. It's not really about sexuality although it is important for us to keep things sexy, as that's how we like it. It's really about beauty and the power of seduction, the things that we believe make fashion more interesting and desirable,' declares Sourigues, who is also a strong advocate of street casting in order to find 'real beauty'.

A flick through Sourigues' image archives reaffirms that desirability exists in spades in his work. Whether it is youthful libido set in action for advertising campaigns for brands such as Pepe Jeans, slick but sensual brand imagery for luxury brand Loewe or editorial stories for *Hercules*, his imagery always ramps up the temperature. Hot girls, hot boys, often in hot locations.

In *Hercules* even androgyny feels the rush, as witnessed in the treatment of the Autumn/Winter 09 story 'Who's that Boy', shot by photographer Paola Kudacki. Famous for her cool, epicene looks, model Iris Strubegger, even when styled in men's tailoring, delivers a potent performance laced with sex and glamour.

While Sourigues' favourite cover is the Autumn/Winter 08 'Tom Ford Five' story, shot by Giampaolo Sgura, and featuring suited and booted Euro dandies in a flamboyant take on the classic country-gent look, the most momentous cover story to date features Brazilian model Raquel Zimmermann, one of the most sought-after models on earth, in full Vegas showgirl mode. Shot by Kudacki, in one image she wears nothing but bunny ears, while on the cover the entire fashion credits go to a pair of nipple tassels, proving that via Sourigues' cleverly crafted touch there is generally as much for the boys (or girls) who like girls as those who like boys. With beauty, seduction and intense physicality the hallmark of *Hercules* (and Sourigues), the issue of persuasion becomes semi-irrelevant.

'Whatever I do, I try to stay loyal to the same values of beauty,' concludes the stylist.

Francesco Sourigues

Pages 178–179
Super-sexualized imagery of the kind *Hercules* revels in, from the story 'I know You Can't Control Yourself Any Longer', photographed by Giampaolo Sgura for the Spring/Summer 2010 issue.

Pages 180–181
Another supermodel, Raquel Zimmerman teams up with Sourigues for the cover story of *Hercules*, photographed by Paola Kudacki for the Spring/Summer 2008 issue.

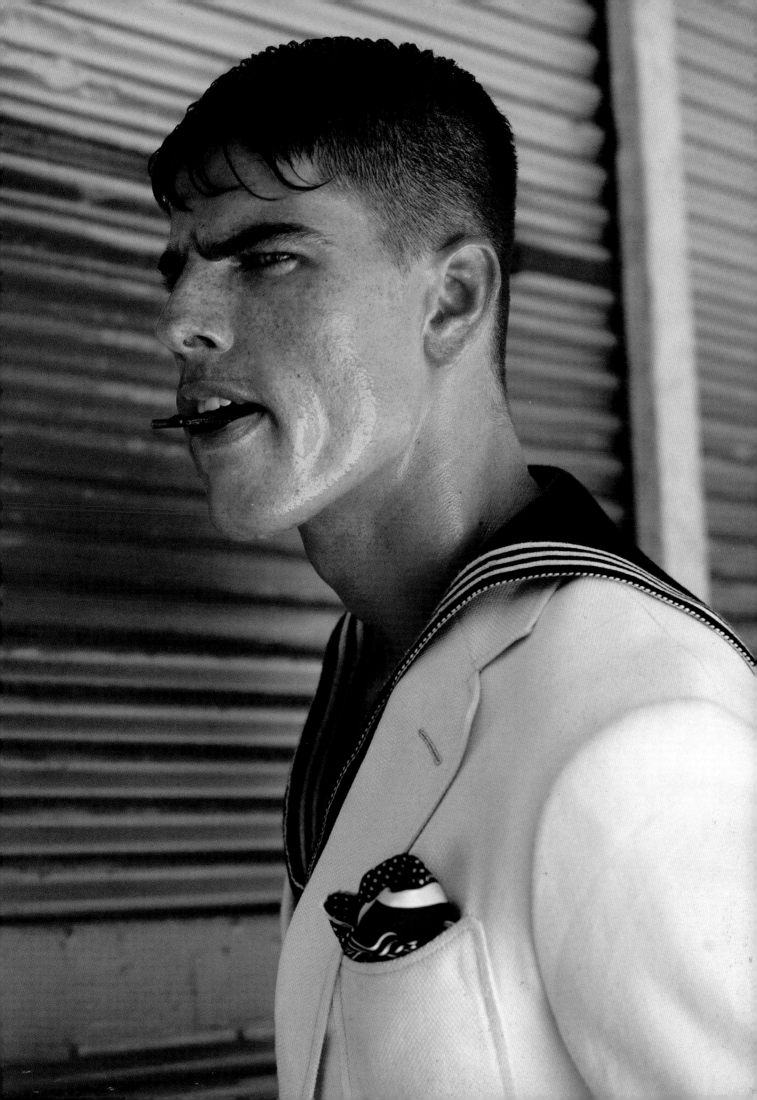

ROBBIE'S
SPENCER

One of fashion's most inspirational new innovators, Robbie Spencer wants to show you something new: essentially the world of fashion informed by almost anything but itself.

'I want to inspire and energize what can, at times, be quite a dull industry,' declares Spencer. 'I'm not really that interested in normality. I want to do something exciting, which makes people think about fashion in another realm. I like the juxtaposition of things when there's an element of normality and then there's also a kind of collision, a clash going on at the same time. It's about highbrow, high aesthetics and I always strive for beauty, even if that's scary or weird. At the end of the day, it's about making a memorable, beautiful image.'

Dedicated to meshing an intellectual or, at the very least, a tangential dimension into the weft of the images he co-authors, Spencer ensures that the first thing that surfaces from any image he touches is an unorthodox approach to just about everything. Maintaining the spirit of the cutting-edge, culturally eclectic style magazine *Dazed & Confused*, with whom he has been an editor since 2004, Spencer is a creative who wants to challenge his audience to reappraise the notion of fashion. Whether it is Daniel Radcliffe on the front cover of *Dazed & Confused* smeared in thirty shades of greasepaint until he is barely recognizable as his family-friendly alter ego Harry Potter, or blonde model Dree Hemingway cast in *Vogue Italia*'s tribute to late fashion icon Isabella Blow, what Spencer does best is use his kaleidoscopic vision (and a provocative slant) to create images that beg fresh questions.

After studying set and interior/spatial design at Chelsea College of Art & Design in London, followed by an environmental arts course at Central Saint Martins College of Art & Design, Spencer switched to London College of Fashion. He enrolled on a degree in fashion promotion, partly to pursue something that would encompass his wider interests, but mostly based on the premise of validating his interest in fashion. 'It was because I'm a bit nerdy,' he explains, 'and I thought at the time that I wanted the certificate, the official recognition, that comes with the certificate.'

It was his assisting job at *Dazed & Confused*, however (by the time Spencer graduated he was already shooting for the magazine outright), that provided the necessary collision of inspiration, artistic freedom and a viable, progressive career, making fashion his perfect fit. 'It's people coming together in this explosion of ideas that's really exciting for me,' says Spencer. 'It's about finding a way to inspire not just readers but designers and the industry as a whole, making people think as differently as possible. You know the trickle-down process Meryl Streep talks about in *The Devil Wears Prada*? That's entirely real.'

With his current tenure at *Dazed & Confused* coinciding with the birth of *Dazed Digital*, the magazine's online platform, Spencer has reached professional maturation hand in hand with a major shift in publishing protocol. With publishing houses grappling for market share and marriages of content and commerce popping up everywhere came the realization that to embrace technology's new horizons and to be able to communicate via a multitude of channels, is key to survival. 'People still want magazines, book-a-zines, things to be inspired by, to archive and look at,' declares Spencer. 'But it's a case of the whole package and for us as stylists or image-makers now, and moving forward, it's about being both multidisciplinary and doing all of these things at the same time.'

As a new breed of stylist, Spencer grasps this multidisciplinary role, delivering an early indication of a seismic shift in the dynamics of the fashion industry's creative hierarchy. Stylists are commissioning photographers, switching to design or even photography themselves and demonstrating a freshly amplified role within the creative master plan.

Spencer asserts the shift: 'I know quite a few photographers who really rely on stylists to come up with directions, directions that they then feel they can work with, as opposed to the other way around. I think every photographer's dream (and I don't mean commercially) is to find someone [a stylist] who is both waiting to be inspired and who can find an idea. That's when you're able to realize it and make their images into something.'

His capacity to harness the outré, like his *Dazed & Confused* predecessors such as Nicola Formichetti and Alister Mackie, has created a folio of images with an exhilarating disregard for conventional fashion in the sense of seasonal trends or safe commercial etiquette. With a nose for tempering the surreal with a degree of simple, personal taste, Spencer is already soaring, by the age of twenty-six, beyond the realms of independent magazines into the exalted fashion stratosphere of *Vogue Italia*, plus taking on creative consultancy roles in Paris, New York and London.

His work with British fashion designer JW Anderson, a designer who similarly likes to pull ideas from beyond fashion (usually historic) into his design language, crystallizes his renunciation of tradition, offering a new code of dressing that is less about androgyny and more about offering a freedom to put boys' clothes on girls and vice versa. The ever-present notion of collision, in this instance of ideas and genders, rises to the surface again. 'I'm still fascinated, and inspired, by the whole context of fashion, way beyond the making of clothes,' stresses Spencer. 'I'm always going to see it as a much broader thing than that. I came into this job as a creative and I'll always remain that way.'

Robbie Spencer

Page 188
Spencer's styling is never just about the clothing. Clockwise from top left: Brit boys punk up a story for *Dazed & Confused* Japan, photographed by Ben Toms, December 2009; models in fetish-style bodysuits for the story 'Masked by a Second Skin', photographed by Kacper Kasprzyk for the February 2010 issue of *Dazed & Confused*; from 'Come Together', a story based on sibling or close connections for the Autumn/Winter 2010 issue of *Vogue Hommes* Japan, photographed by Ben Toms; an extract from the 'War Hero' story, for the July 2010 issue of *Dazed & Confused,* photographed by Richard Burbridge.

Page 189
Also from *Dazed & Confused*'s October 2009 'Franken-Fashion' issue, photographed by Richard Burbridge.

MELANIE WARD·

Melanie Ward

Page 191
Actress Charlotte
Gainsbourg in the
'Portrait of a Lady' story,
for *Harper's Bazaar*
US, November 2000,
photographed by
Inez & Vinoodh.

'I am not a fan of clothing that screams fashion. It has always been about an effortless look for me, an allure, an attitude with a little twist to make it personal,' declares arch-modernist Melanie Ward. Ward is a creative whose boundary-pushing curiosity and passion for style with real substance changed the shape of fashion so dramatically in the 1990s that she has been an icon for a legion of fashion subversives (and enthusiasts) ever since.

'My tastes are constantly evolving, but one thing that always defines me is a certain irreverence towards clothes,' says British-born Ward. 'I'm not afraid to just rip into something with my scissors. I like to be surprised and to surprise myself. I am much more interested in the mix of things that define personal style than trends that originate in the past. I prefer to live in the now.'

The industry has always kept a beady eye on wherever Ward's 'now' is. Her accolades include muse and collaborator for Helmut Lang, creative director for Karl Lagerfeld's eponymous line, design consultant for Jil Sander, Calvin Klein and a multitude of other luxury brands plus senior fashion editor of *Harper's Bazaar* US. Her ability to mix ideas and redefine existing concepts in her own inimitable way epitomizes what the very best moments in fashion are often made of: originality, subversion and an enticing glimpse of what the future might hold.

As a direct legacy of a childhood characterized by creative self-expression alongside intellectual endeavour, Ward's fertile vision has long been trained on making transient ideas tangible. Influenced by her mother, who had her own clothes made for her, Ward found a natural logic in the notion of carving something from nothing. 'Sweaters became twisted pencil skirts; men's blazers became minidresses. I went through a black phase and dyed everything black in my parent's saucepans!'

Educated by nuns until she was eighteen, Ward first studied politics and languages at the University of London, but the impulse to create was so strong that she continued to design, essentially moonlighting as her own personal dressmaker in the evenings. 'I kind of lived two parallel lives,' says Ward. 'By day I studied Machiavelli, Zola and Sartre and by night I made clothes for myself.' She formalized that impulse following her degree by studying fashion at Central Saint Martins College of Art & Design, where her debut collection was awarded the prize for Best Daywear.

It was in the late 1980s and early 1990s, however, when Ward first made her presence felt globally, as part of a new creative vanguard of pioneering British image-makers such as David Sims and Corinne Day. Looking to communicate a spirit attuned to the imperfect beauty they saw around them, they defiantly broke through the unfeasibly glossy artifice constructed by decades of glamazons cavorting through the pages of *Vogue* and *Harper's Bazaar*, instead using style magazines such as *i-D* and *The Face* to showcase a new vision of fashion: the grunge movement.

It was an instinctual call-to-action that signalled the death knell for fashion's one-track vision of flawless glamour, and the subsequent influx of a new wave of modern muses – imperfect yet equally alluring beauties such as Kate Moss – who would be instrumental in setting fashion's new course. It was a visionary perspective, which struck a chord with both those inside and beyond the fashion industry. *The Face*'s now-iconic July 1990 cover story entitled 'The Third Summer of Love', shot by Day and featuring a fifteen-year-old Kate Moss with no make-up, spoke a thousand words, distilling the essence of an era into a single shot. Revelling in youthful hedonism, it defined the voice of an entire generation looking for something real with which to identify.

'There were no rules that we adhered to; we were fearless and inspired,' recalls Ward. 'David Sims and I set up backdrops on the fire ecape of a London studio. Corinne Day, Kate and I spent freezing afternoons on dreary English beaches and streets....My belief in effortless dressing as defined initially by the grunge days remains one of my core leitmotifs to this day.'

The notion of the perfect imperfect holds a deep resonance for Ward, who has always endeavoured to maintain a high level of honesty and integrity throughout her work. In editorial stories for magazines such as *i-D*, *The Face* and *L'Uomo Vogue*, Ward would defy convention by reworking the garments herself, pairing silk gowns with trainers or pushing a pair of jeans lower on the hips than was the norm in order to subvert the intended silhouette. That thread of experimentation still permeates her editorial work to this day. The pre-Oscars-based story 'Best Performances', shot by Inez and Vinoodh in the February 2011 issue of *W* magazine, depicts actors including Helena Bonham Carter, Colin Firth and Nicole Kidman visually teetering further out of the generic celebrity comfort zone than ever captured before. The famously clean-cut Kidman looks uncharacteristically dishevelled and sexy in a ripped T-shirt held together with safety pins (another residual echo of the early years). Visual showmanship underscores the story but a sense of humanity remains equally as strong.

'On reflection, most of my muses tend to be somewhat defiant, with a strong sense of self and their sexuality,' reveals Ward. 'But there is always a human element in my work. I like things that are a little off. I love to make things come undone. Imperfection is very sexy and modern to me.'

This sharply executed edginess and increasingly unfussy aesthetic swiftly drew a swathe of high-profile designers towards her, all eager to assimilate her creative credibility in to their own collections. From 1992 to 1995, Ward collaborated with the queen of minimalist luxury, German designer Jil Sander, directly followed in 1995 (the same year Ward moved from London to New York to work for *Harper's Bazaar*) by American fashion titan Calvin Klein. For a designer for whom operating on the cusp of modernity was the axis on which his entire business turned, Ward was the perfect fit. It was, indeed, for Klein that she reprised her partnership with Kate Moss on the now-legendary then-controversial CK jeans campaign. 'I loved collaborating with Melanie because she always brought her great taste, creativity, intelligence and her sense of modernity to styling many of my collections and advertising campaigns,' affirms Klein.

Having spent thirteen years as collaborator and muse of Helmut Lang, followed by another high-profile position as creative director of Karl Lagerfeld, in 2009 Ward finally rallied the vast design vocabulary she had amassed into her own capsule collection – Blouson Noir – that garnered considerable acclaim from international press and buyers alike. She remains a beacon of modernity no matter which avenue she turns her skills to, apparently still propelled by the need to test her own instincts and curiosity. 'My whole career to date has evolved in a very organic way,' says Ward. 'Everything has come from my gut and my heart, never my head.'

Melanie Ward

Page 194
From stylist to designer, a Spring/Summer 2010 look-book image from Ward's fashion label Blouson Noir. Photographed by Inez & Vinoodh.

Page 195
An iconic image of a fifteen-year-old Kate Moss, photographed by Corinne Day for 'The Third Summer of Love' issue of *The Face*, published in 1990. The story defined the era and changed the face of fashion forever.

PATTI WILSON

Patti Wilson

Pages 196–197

An unpublished image originally photographed by Sølve Sundsbø for *Vogue Italia*.

Page 199

Model Constance Jablonski is transported into a different fashion dimension via Wilson's extravagant imagination. Photographed by Greg Kadel for the October 2010 issue of *Numero* magazine.

From jazz-club hostess to contributing editor for the holy grail of all editorial fashion, *Vogue Italia*, the career trajectory of charismatic stylist Patti Wilson is as fantastical and inspiring as the legions of spectacular images that accompany her.

Wilson's fashion story, now the stuff of industry legend, began when she was plucked from relative obscurity by a fashion photographer intrigued by the wild outfits she was wearing – outfits that Wilson describes as 'pure Billie Holiday' – while waitressing in a New York jazz bar. Slipping into styling like a second skin, the native New Yorker spent several years assisting before eventually catching the attention of celebrated photographers Bill King (the first major photographer to take Wilson on), Art Kane and Sarah Moon. It was a combination of photographers whose ability to smoothly shape-shift between the worlds of fashion, art and music that would form the genesis of Wilson's career proper – instilling in her an understanding of how to not only impress but also send messages with imagery.

The inextricable connections to all veins of creative culture that permeated the photographers' work remain a strong influence on Wilson's aesthetic, but it was her inspired, if creatively fraught, partnership with controversial photographer David LaChapelle that propelled her into the spotlight. Bearing traces of the maverick spirit visualized by art director Jean-Paul Goude, theirs was a chemistry based on mischief, a shared passion for prowling through the annals of pop culture and the stiff mutual challenge each faced from the other. Negotiating a creative tug-of-war, Wilson took the visually extravagant cultural delirium concocted by LaChapelle and completed the picture, quite literally, by saturating it with high fashion.

'That's where David and I were genius,' explains Wilson, 'because he was more of an artist and I was in fashion. It was such a challenge, so crazy. It was insane in his studio – the way he would conjure up things and he would change his stuff right in the middle, bringing in something completely off the wall. He'd say to me "ugh, I don't want to shoot that credit", so I would never tell him and just drag it in because I loved my role at *Vogue Italia*. It was weird but it worked. Although there were times where I used to get embarrassed and say I didn't do it.'

At the time, the duo's fantastical images were often deemed too outrageous for mainstream magazines to take them on, but a shift in perception – spearheaded by the trailblazing British style magazine *i-D*, whose own language as a platform for the new and the subversive carried an affinity with the LaChapelle/Wilson partnership – led to a position of critical notoriety and ultimate validation. As a conduit to the global stage, the *i-D* seal of approval fed the pair directly into the equally coveted worlds of *Vanity Fair, Harper's Bazaar* US, *Vogue Paris* and *Vogue Italia*, marking Wilson's transition into high fashion's international super leagues. Courtesy of continued support from editor-in-chief of *Vogue Italia* Franca Sozzani, industry powerhouses Steven Meisel and Steven Klein came calling (later joined by fashion greats Terry Richardson, Peter Lindbergh, Miles Aldridge, Tom Munro, Paolo Roversi and Sølve Sundsbø), and Wilson's place in the pantheon of fashion's elite was secured.

The fresh energy Wilson found in the partnership with Klein in particular, progressed the development of the dynamic visual language she had cultivated with LaChapelle, but she exchanged the outrageous exuberance of her previous partner's outré humour for Klein's powerful, sensuous and often epic visual narratives. 'I love working with Steven because he brings tension to the fashion,' says Wilson. 'He brings an emotion that

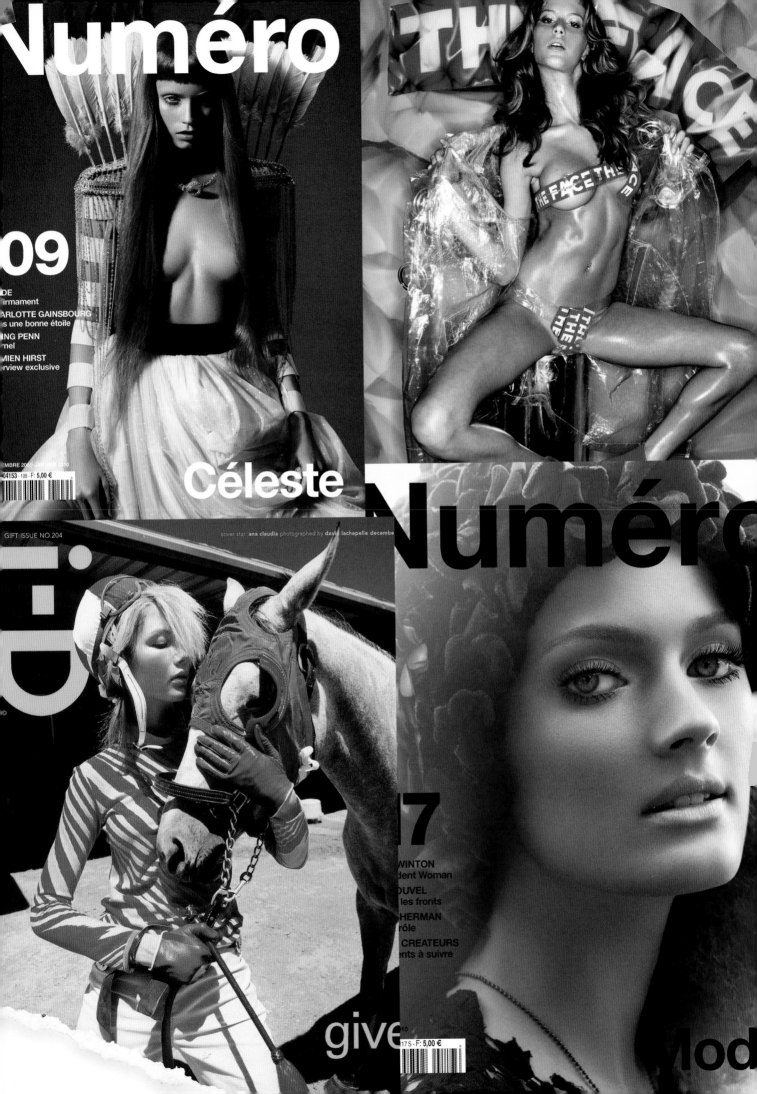

Numéro

09

DE
irmament

ARLOTTE GAINSBOURG
s une bonne étoile

NG PENN
nel

MIEN HIRST
rview exclusive

EMBRE 2009-JANVIER 2010

04153 - 109 - F: 5,00 €

Céleste

GIFT ISSUE NO.204

cover star: ana claudia photographed by david lachapelle decembe

Numéro

7

WINTON
dent Woman

OUVEL
les fronts

HERMAN
rôle

CREATEURS
ents à suivre

give

17 S - F: 5,00 €

Mod

nobody else can grab. It's something beyond clothes. It makes every-thing interesting because how much of the clothes can you really see? He derives an emotion from the clothes that is extraordinary.'

Whether striding through the city, holding court at the side of a public swimming pool or prowling the edges of a parking lot, Wilson's and Klein's characters, every one a mistress of high fashion, have come to epitomize *Vogue Italia*'s trademark: strong, sensual, iconic imagery. Wilson's contribution to the characterization, fuelled by research pulled from film and music, ensures that each one leaps from the page like a creature from a parallel universe. They lap up every nuance of the high drama of fashion and it is virtually impossible to draw a line between when the styling stops and the image-making takes over.

As fashion in the extreme – brilliant, beautiful, entertaining and always memorable – it is exactly what has endeared Wilson to countless fashion houses, cosmetic brands, musicians and actors seeking a larger, more exciting visual narrative with which to enrich their story. From Christian Dior (for whom Wilson created a short film with director David Lynch and actress Marion Cotillard) to denim brand Pepe, to have Wilson is to have invaluable access to an indefatigable energy and an unfettered imagination.

Testament to Wilson's boundless energy and her thirst for new avenues of inspiration is her continual support of new design talent. Despite her stellar status and an almost windowless schedule, Wilson also styles shows for rising star, New York designer Rad Hourani – a talent whom she spotted during her biannual scouting sessions at the New York shows.

Continual collaborations with emerging photographic talent have also helped Wilson – a stylist who never divulges her age and claims her strongest motivation comes from searching for the next new thing – to side-step the professional pitfall of losing relevance. Her description of a recent shoot with an anonymous young photographer sums up both Wilson's tenacity and her endless passion. 'His nonchalance was killing me,' she says of the photographer, 'but I'd work with him in a heartbeat again.'

Patti Wilson

Page 200
Wilson's infectious energy has produced some of the most vibrant and influential cover art of the last decade. Clockwise from top left: *Numero*, December 2009, photographed by Miguel Reveriego; supermodel Gisele Bundchen, photographed by David LaChapelle for *The Face*, 2000; the October 2010 issue of *Numero*, photographed by Greg Kadel; *i-D*'s 'Gift' issue, December 2000.

Pages 202–203
Wilson transforms model Karen Elson for the 'Mad Magic Magnificent!' story, photographed by Steven Klein for the March 2004 issue of *Vogue Italia*.

Contacts

Christiane Arp
www.vogue.de

Camille Bidault-Waddington
Management Artists
www.managementartists.com
maoparis@managementartists.com
maony@managementartists.com
T: +33 1 4271 6060 (Paris)
T: +1 212 931 9311 (New York)

Judy Blame
CLM
www.clmuk.com
T: +44 20 7313 8310 (London)
T: +1 212 924 6565 (New York)
T: +1 917 443 2019 (Los Angeles)

David Bradshaw
georgina@davidbradshaw.co.uk

Francesca Burns
www.vogue.co.uk

Leith Clark
D&V Management
www.dandvmanagement.com
T: +44 20 7372 2555 (London)

Marie Chaix
CLM

Anna Dello Russo
Innovative Fashion Ideas
www.innovativefashionideas.com
www.annadellorusso.com
europe@innovativefashionideas.com
T: +39 0 245 470 950 (Milan)

Markus Ebner
www.achtung-mode.com
post@achtung-mode.com
T: +49 30 44 01 35 67 (Berlin)

Katy England
Intrepid London
www.intrepidlondon.com
anya@intrepidlondon.com
T: +44 20 7485 9372 (London)

Edward Enninful
Maxim Fashion Agents
www.maximfma.com
info-fashion@maximfma.com
T: +44 20 8969 6655 (London)
T: +1 212 905 7701 (New York)

Nicola Formichetti
CLM
www.clmuk.com
www.nicolaformichetti.com

Simon Foxton
CLM

Katie Grand
CLM

Jacob K
Streeters London
www.streeters.com
info@streeterslondon.com
T: +44 20 7253 3949/3330 (London)

Alister Mackie
Streeters London

Sophia Neophitou-Apostolou
www.10magazine.com
T: +44 20 7434 0042 (London)

Marie-Amélie Sauvé
Art+Commerce
www.artandcommerce.com
artists@artandcommerce.com
T: +1 212 206 0737 (New York)
T: +33 1 7490 5050 (Paris)

Venetia Scott
CLM

Katie Shillingford
Intrepid London

Tabitha Simmons
Streeters New York
www.streeters.com
info@streetersnewyork.com
T: +1 212 219 9566 (New York)

Francesco Sourigues
www.herculesmag.com
fashion@herculesmag.com

Robbie Spencer
Intrepid London

Melanie Ward
The Collective Shift
www.thecollectiveshift.com
contact@thecollectiveshift.com
T: +1 212 226 1544 (New York)

Patti Wilson
The Collective Shift

Picture Credits

The author and publisher would like to thank the following for providing images for use in this book. In all cases, every effort has been made to credit the copyright holders, but should there be any omissions or errors the publisher would be pleased to insert the appropriate acknowledgement in any subsequent edition of this book (t = top, b = bottom, l = left, r = right):

p 2 Craig McDean/ Art+Commerce

p 7 Nick Knight/ trunkarchive.com

pp 11–17 All images courtesy of Condé Nast Germany

p 22 tr Terry Richardson/ Art Partner

p 23 Glen Luchford/ Art Partner

pp 24–25 Glen Luchford/ Art Partner

p 33 Sølve Sundsbø/ Art+Commerce

p 38 David Sims/ Art Partner

p 42 all Nathaniel Golberg/ Art+Commerce

pp 44–45 Model: Hannah Holman@ Elite NY, hair&make-up: Osvaldo Salvatierra@ Streeters NY. Shot on location at Hannah's home in Utah

pp 50–51 Alasdair McLellan/Art Partner

p 53 Sølve Sundsbø/ Art+Commerce

p 54 Hans Feurer/ Vogue Paris

p 55 t Richard Burbridge/ Art+Commerce

p 55 bl & br Courtesy of Proenza Schouler

pp 58–59 Richard Burbridge/ Art+Commerce

p 67 ©The Helmut Newton Estate/ Maconochie Photography

p 80 Nick Knight/ trunkarchive.com

p 83 Nick Knight/ trunkarchive.com

pp 84–85 Mario Sorrenti/Art Partner

pp 86–87 catwalking.com

p 93 tl Richard Burbridge/ Art+Commerce

pp 94–95 Sølve Sundsbø/ Art+Commerce

pp 98–99 Pictures: Mariano Vivanco, Model Rick Genest for Mugler menswear AW11/12

p 100 Courtesy of Condé Nast Japan

p 101 bl Cover Image Courtesy of *Rolling Stone* Issue Dated July 8–22, 2010 © *Rolling Stone* LLC 2010 All rights reserved. Reprinted by permission of *Rolling Stone* LLC

p 101 br Mario Testino/ Art Partner

pp 102–103 Sølve Sundsbø/ Art+Commerce

p 106 br Nick Knight/ trunkarchive.com

p 109 Alasdair McLellan/Art Partner

pp 113, 115 LOVE © The Condé Nast Publications Ltd

pp 118–119 Courtesy of Louis Vuitton

pp 120–121 Paolo Roversi/ Art+Commerce

pp 128–129 Nick Knight/ trunkarchive.com

p 131 all Nick Knight/ trunkarchive.com

p 133 Nick Knight/ trunkarchive.com

p 140 t Cedric Buchet/ Art Partner

p 145 David Sims/ Art Partner

p 147 David Sims/ Art Partner

pp 148–149 David Sims/ Art Partner. Models: Suvi at Next and Anabela at Silent

p 151 David Sims/ Art Partner

p 161 Hair: Duffy@ Tim Howard, make-up: Lisa Houghton@ Jet Root inc for YSL, set design: Matt Mazzucca@ Rassa Montaser, models: Karolina Kurkova@ IMG, Julia Stenger@ IMG, Ana Beatriz Barros@ Elite Models

p 164 tl Hair: Raphael Salley, make-up: Ayami Nishimura, set design: Gary Card

pp 166–167 Craig McDean/ Art+Commerce

p 170 all Craig McDean/ Art+Commerce

p 171 Inez & Vinoodh/ trunkarchive.com

p 172 Mario Sorrenti/ Art Partner

p 173 Craig McDean/ Art+Commerce

p 175 Paola Kudacki/ trunkarchive.com

pp 180–181 Paola Kudacki/ trunkarchive.com

p 183 Richard Burbridge/ Art+Commerce

p 186 Collage by James West

p 187 Collier Schorr/ 303 Gallery

p 188 bl Richard Burbridge/ Art+Commerce

p 189 Richard Burbridge/ Art+Commerce

p 191 Inez & Vinoodh/ trunkarchive.com

p 194 Inez & Vinoodh/ trunkarchive.com

p 195 Courtesy of the Corinne Day Estate and Gimpel Fils

pp 196–197 Sølve Sundsbø/ Art+Commerce

p 199 Greg Kadel/ trunkarchive.com

p 200 tl Miguel Reveriego/ trunkarchive.com

p 200 tr David LaChapelle/ Art+Commerce

p 200 bl David LaChapelle/ Art+Commerce

p 200 br Greg Kadel/ trunkarchive.com

pp 202–203 Steven Klein/kleinstudio.us

Author's Acknowledgements

A special thanks to all the stylists and photographers whose time, energy and extraordinary vision made this book possible.

For their invaluable input:

Peter Lindbergh, Olivier Zahm, Italo Zucchelli, Neville Brody, Roland Mouret, Jack McCollough & Lazaro Hernandez, Walter Pfeiffer, Mario Sorrenti, Kate Moss, Lady Gaga, Jason Evans, Marc Jacobs, Victoria Beckham, Roland Mouret, Antonio Berardi, Nicolas Ghesquiére, Juergen Teller, Gareth Pugh, Anna Wintour, Calvin Klein.

I would also like to thank the following individuals for their endless support and belief in this project: Ben Cox, Evi Peroulaki, Helen Rochester, Zoe Antoniou, Fiona Harkin, Faye McLeod, Nick Knight, Charlotte Knight, Georgina Talbot, Tracy Le Marquand, Rosie Savile, Birgitta Toyoda, Kathryn Scahill, Cassandra Maxwell, Christine Lavigne, Cale Harrison, Thomas Bonnouvrier, Elodie Touboul David, Alexandre Lamare, Liz McKiver, Lauren Switzer, Charlotte Alexa, Carla Pierce, Laurence Kleinknecht, Antony Miles, Ines Thomas, Micha Weidmann and Christopher Michael.

Index

Page numbers in bold refer to pictures